What is Latin American History?

What is History? series

John H. Arnold, *What is Medieval History?* 2nd edition

Peter Burke, *What is Cultural History?* 3rd edition

Peter Burke, *What is the History of Knowledge?*

John C. Burnham, *What is Medical History?*

Pamela Kyle Crossley, *What is Global History?*

Pero Gaglo Dagbovie, *What is African American History?*

Marshall C. Eakin, *What is Latin American History?*

Shane Ewen, *What is Urban History?*

Christiane Harzig and Dirk Hoerder, with Donna Gabaccia, *What is Migration History?*

J. Donald Hughes, *What is Environmental History?* 2nd edition

Andrew Leach, *What is Architectural History?*

Stephen Morillo with Michael F. Pavkovic, *What is Military History?* 3rd edition

James Raven, *What is the History of the Book?*

Sonya O. Rose, *What is Gender History?*

Barbara H. Rosenwein and Riccardo Cristiani, *What is the History of Emotions?*

Hannu Salmi, *What is Digital History?*

Brenda E. Stevenson, *What is Slavery?*

Jeffrey Weeks, *What is Sexual History?*

Richard Whatmore, *What is Intellectual History?*

Merry Wiesner-Hanks, *What is Early Modern History?*

What is Latin American History?

Marshall C. Eakin

polity

Copyright © Marshall C. Eakin 2021

The right of Marshall C. Eakin to be identified as Author of this Work has been asserted in accordance with the UK Copyright, Designs and Patents Act 1988.

First published in 2021 by Polity Press

Polity Press
65 Bridge Street
Cambridge CB2 1UR, UK

Polity Press
101 Station Landing
Suite 300
Medford, MA 02155, USA

All rights reserved. Except for the quotation of short passages for the purpose of criticism and review, no part of this publication may be reproduced, stored in a retrieval system or transmitted, in any form or by any means, electronic, mechanical, photocopying, recording or otherwise, without the prior permission of the publisher.

ISBN-13: 978-1-5095-3851-5
ISBN-13: 978-1-5095-3852-2 (pb)

A catalogue record for this book is available from the British Library.
Library of Congress Cataloging-in-Publication Data

Names: Eakin, Marshall C. (Marshall Craig), 1952- author.
Title: What is Latin American history? / Marshall C. Eakin.
Description: Cambridge, UK ; Medford, MA : Polity, 2021. | Series: What is history? | Includes bibliographical references and index. | Summary: "The first student-friendly guide to the sub-field of Latin American history"-- Provided by publisher.
Identifiers: LCCN 2021006121 (print) | LCCN 2021006122 (ebook) | ISBN 9781509538515 | ISBN 9781509538522 (pb) | ISBN 9781509538539 (epub)
Subjects: LCSH: Latin America--Historiography. | Historians--Latin America. | Latin America--History--20th century.
Classification: LCC F1409.7 .E24 2021 (print) | LCC F1409.7 (ebook) | DDC 980.03--dc23
LC record available at https://lccn.loc.gov/2021006121
LC ebook record available at https://lccn.loc.gov/2021006122

Typeset in 10.5 on 12pt Sabon
by Fakenham Prepress Solutions, Fakenham, Norfolk NR21 8NL
Printed and bound in the UK by CPI Group (UK) Ltd, Croydon

The publisher has used its best endeavours to ensure that the URLs for external websites referred to in this book are correct and active at the time of going to press. However, the publisher has no responsibility for the websites and can make no guarantee that a site will remain live or that the content is or will remain appropriate.

Every effort has been made to trace all copyright holders, but if any have been overlooked the publisher will be pleased to include any necessary credits in any subsequent reprint or edition.

For further information on Polity, visit our website:
politybooks.com

Contents

Acknowledgments		vii
Introduction		1
1	What Is Latin America?	5
2	The Pioneering Generations	19
3	The Economic and Quantitative Turns	36
4	The Social Turn	51
5	Cultural and Other Turns	75
6	Beyond Latin American History	96
Epilogue: The Future of Latin American History		121
Notes		127
Further Reading		151
Index		156

Acknowledgments

I would like to thank Pascal Porcheron and Polity Press for the invitation to write this book. Although I have long reflected on the history of Latin American history, and have even written a bit about the subject, writing this volume has given me the opportunity to take a closer and deeper look at the *longue durée* of the field. I have been a participant-observer over the past five decades in the shifting historiographical approaches I describe in chapters 3–6. Revisiting this history has been an enlightening personal as well as professional encounter with Latin American history and historians across decades and centuries.

An *abraço* to Tom Holloway for his advice and suggestions since the inception of the project. I also very much appreciate the generous and helpful comments of the two anonymous outside readers of the manuscript. Many, many years ago, Teresa Meade (without either of us knowing) gave me the initial push in our work on the Conference on Latin American History's Teaching Committee. *Obrigado*, Teresa. After a quarter century, here is the result of our discussions. As always, many thanks to my colleagues in the Department of History at Vanderbilt University, especially Jane Landers, Celso Castilho, Eddie Wright-Rios, and Frank Robinson, our Latin American history *junta*. The graduate students in my Research Seminar in Latin American History during the fall of 2020 read and discussed an earlier version of the manuscript. Thank you, Claudia Monterroza Rivera, André Ramos Chacón, Ricky Sakamoto-Pugh, and Alex Sanchez.

Finally, my thanks to Pascal and his able crew – Ellen MacDonald-Kramer, Stephanie Homer, Rachel Moore, and Caroline Richmond – who have shepherded the project from inception to completion.

Introduction

Latin American history has become a vibrant and dynamic field of study over the last half-century even as historians of Latin America have found it increasingly difficult to agree on how to define the region they study. As the field has become more and more professionalized and specialized, some of the most influential and innovative work on the region crosses multiple political and cultural boundaries, often stretching thematically and geographically into other areas of the world. The field began to emerge a century ago, largely out of work inspired by national histories written by Latin Americans and of a few historians in the United States and Europe, whose work was often shaped by the power of their own countries in Latin America and the world. Today, in an age of rapid globalization and transnational exchanges, Latin American history is a highly developed field within the historical profession, but it will become more difficult in the coming decades to speak of something we can call Latin America. The end of Latin America as a coherent region and object of study could be the future of Latin American history.

In the United States the professionalization of Latin American history began at the close of the nineteenth century, grew slowly in the first half of the twentieth century, and emerged as a dynamic and substantial professional field in the last decades of the twentieth century. The Conference on Latin American History, the primary professional association of historians of Latin America in the United States, counted more than one thousand members in the first two decades of the twenty-first century. (As a point of comparison, the membership of the American Historical Association in 2020 was about 12,000.) A much smaller but important community of historians emerged simultaneously in Great Britain and Canada, and a very small but excellent group had taken shape in Australia by 2000. Much as in Great Britain, there is a small community of historians of Latin America across Europe, most notably in Spain, Portugal, France, and Germany.

Latin Americans, not surprisingly, have produced the vast majority of historical writing on Latin America. Until the second half of the twentieth century, writers who were rarely professional or university-based historians produced most of this work. With the rise of universities and graduate programs since the Second World War, nearly all the nations of Latin America now generate a steady stream of professional historians with university positions who publish in a vast array of professional journals and with many publishers. Despite a growing trend after 1950 toward a greater awareness of work across national boundaries, overwhelmingly the publications of historians in Latin America focus on the history of their own nation or some part of their nation. In Brazil alone, for example, by 2010 university graduate programs generated more than 1,000 M.A. theses and 300 doctoral dissertations per year, the vast majority on the history of Brazil. In short, there are striking asymmetries in the production of work on the history of Latin America. In the United States, with its enormous and highly developed university doctoral programs, more than 170 in history alone, historians of Latin America make up about 7 percent of the profession and produce around 75 doctoral dissertations annually. In Mexico and Brazil, both with highly developed graduate programs in history, probably above 80 percent of the academic historians work on their native country.

This short book traces the development of the field of Latin American history with an emphasis both on recent decades and on Anglophone scholarship, for two key reasons. First, its principal audience is in the United States and the United Kingdom. Second, the historical literature produced in Latin

America is so vast and diverse that it would be impossible for one historian (from anywhere in the region) to do it justice. Throughout this volume, I will discuss trends in the United States, Europe, and Latin America, but the emphasis is on work in English. In the endnotes, I note some examples of key works, but I do not attempt to be comprehensive in my citations.

One of the objectives of the historian is to attempt, however imperfectly, to recover the past to understand who we are by seeing from whence we came. Who we are – as individuals, societies, nations – bears the traces of decades, centuries, even millennia of historical processes and events. Contemporary Latin America cannot be understood without a deep knowledge of at least five centuries of these processes and events. In this slim volume, this historian turns to the past to understand the field of Latin American history, its origins, patterns, and multiple paths. Just as one cannot understand Latin America today without the long view of how we arrived at this moment, the historian of Latin America cannot fully appreciate the field without looking back over the decades and centuries to appreciate the many converging and diverging paths. This is a field that has long been open to influences from multiple disciplines and approaches on multiple continents. My hope is that this brief survey provides some insights into the creation, development, complexities, and fragmentation of the field of Latin American history.

The first chapter grapples with a central conundrum – how to define this region called Latin America. Those in the humanities and social sciences who study this region cannot even agree on a definition of the term. Increasingly, those in cultural studies have argued that the very notion of a region called Latin America is an illusion, one created out of imperial and Cold War struggles, a term flawed from the beginning, and one that we should discard. Chapter 2 then traces the origins of the field in the work of what I call "gentlemen scholars" in the nineteenth century and the growth of small academic communities in North America, Europe, and a few nations of Latin America before the First World War. The professional field in the United States begins to emerge gradually in the first half of the twentieth century and, by the 1950s, the Cuban Revolution and U.S. responses to the rise of leftist revolution in Latin America spurred a boom in Latin American studies. The following four chapters are largely thematic with a touch of chronological order. In the 1960s and 1970s, the historical profession, in general, and Latin American history, in particular, took a social and economic turn. Historians moved away from the history of high politics, diplomacy, and warfare to emphasize social classes, "history from below," and quantification. Structure came into vogue as historians of Latin America counted, tabulated, and computed prices, wages, and economic indicators and sought to uncover foundational economic and social structures. Chapters 3 and 4 look at the social and economic turns.

By the late 1980s, the wave of social and economic history, especially quantification, faded, and (along with much of the profession) historians of Latin America took the so-called cultural turn, especially in the United States. Shunning structures and meta-narratives, they honed in on identities, race, ethnicity, and cultural analysis. Rather than constructing narratives of nations and structures, they turned to agency and micro-history. Chapter 5 analyzes these trends. Chapter 6 turns to the diverse trends within Latin American history over the past two decades. The dominance of the cultural turn has eased as new forms of social and political history have emerged. An emphasis on the imperial, transnational, regional, and global has emerged, represented most dramatically by fields such as borderlands and Atlantic world history. Most striking has been the continually rising production and expansion of the academic communities in Latin America over the last two generations. In the epilog, I return to the idea of Latin America, the increasing diversity of the countries and peoples in the region, and the challenges of writing the history of Latin America in the future.

1
What Is Latin America?

Latin America is a conundrum, a statement that applies to both the region and the name. The dimensions of the region are unclear, the name a misnomer, and, for some, the place does not even exist. Thousands of scholars on several continents study Latin America. In the United States, the broader field of Latin American studies has been vibrant and growing for decades. Every four years, the U.S. Department of Education awards millions of dollars to about fifteen "national resource centers" in Latin American studies. Yet, no one seems to like the name for this region of the world, and a growing number of academics have even declared that the very idea of Latin America is a fiction invented by European and American elites. If they are correct, the field of Latin American history is an illusion. Even those who argue for the usefulness of the term (despite its flaws) cannot agree on a definition of just what it encompasses. Moreover, as the many nations in the region continue to develop in the twenty-first century, it will be increasingly difficult to discern strong similarities that hold them together as a coherent and meaningful regional unit. In short, we may be able to speak of Latin America's history, but it may not have much of a future.

The name Latin America, or, more precisely in Spanish and Portuguese, *América Latina*, does not even appear in print until the mid-nineteenth century. Three hundred and fifty years earlier, when Christopher Columbus came ashore on the islands of what he called *El Mar Caribe* (the Caribbean Sea), he firmly believed that he had arrived on the eastern shores of the Indies (Japan and China). A German cartographer, Martin Waldseemüller, produced one of the first maps of the region in 1507. He had read the accounts of Florentine navigator Amerigo Vespucci's transatlantic voyages, believed he had discovered this new world, and proceeded to designate this "new" landmass America in his honor. The great cartographer later regretted his error and removed the designation from his maps, but the name has stuck with us now for more than five centuries.

The lands and peoples of the Americas presented a major intellectual challenge for Europeans. They did not appear in the two most important authorities in Western civilization, the Bible and the classical writings of the Greeks and Romans. For many decades after the "Columbian Moment" the Europeans would puzzle over how to explain their absence from these foundational sources and how to fit them into their worldview.[1] Were these "Indians" descendants of the Lost Tribes of Israel? Were they humans? Did they have souls? Europeans often referred to the Americas as the "New World" to differentiate it from the "Old World" of Europe, Africa, and Asia, continents they had long known. The Spanish crown gradually created a vast bureaucracy to govern their new colonies as they took shape and, following Columbus, called the region the Indies (*las Indias*).

This vast geographical region of North, Central, and South America and the Caribbean was home to possibly 75 million or more native peoples in 1492, peoples Columbus (mistakenly) called Indians (*indios*), another name that stuck. The Native American population declined dramatically, possibly by as much as 75 to 90 percent in the sixteenth century, largely from diseases that arrived from Europe and Africa (smallpox, measles, influenza, plague, malaria, yellow fever). The populations of indigenous peoples began slowly to recover from this staggering demographic catastrophe in the seventeenth century. During four centuries of conquest and colonial rule, Europeans brought at least 12 million Africans across the Atlantic in chains to provide enslaved labor on plantations and in mines, and to work in nearly every aspect of colonial life. Slave traders shipped the vast majority of these Africans (around 80 to 85 percent) into the Caribbean basin and eastern Brazil. Probably fewer than 1,500 Spaniards and Portuguese per year arrived in the region over the course of the sixteenth century and during the remainder of the colonial period. Consequently, when the wars for independence erupted in the early nineteenth century, the estimated 25 million inhabitants of the region probably consisted of about 15 million Native Americans, about 3 million people of European descent, 2 million enslaved people of African descent, and about 5 million people of racially mixed heritage. Even after three centuries of colonialism and exploitation, more than half the inhabitants of what we now call Latin America were Native Americans, and only a little over 10 percent were persons who claimed European (or Latin) ancestry. The vast lands the Spanish and Portuguese claimed stretched from what today is the southern tier of the United States (California to Florida) to Tierra del Fuego. With the rise of the French, English, and Dutch empires after 1600, these European powers seized control of many Caribbean islands (such as Jamaica, Barbados, Saint-Domingue, and Curaçao) and enclaves on the American mainland (such as the Guianas, Belize, and, eventually, Louisiana).

By the eighteenth century, those of Spanish descent born in the Americas increasingly referred to themselves as creoles (*criollos*) to distinguish themselves from Spaniards born in Spain but residing in the Americas (*peninsulares*). Although those of Portuguese descent in Brazil were cognizant of their differences with those born in Portugal, the social distinctions were less pronounced than those between the *criollos* and *peninsulares*. Europeans and Euro-Americans sometimes referred to their regions as *América española* or *América portuguesa*. As the Euro-Americans fought to break with their colonial masters in the early nineteenth century, they contrasted themselves with the Europeans and began to call themselves *americanos* or, in the case of the Spanish colonies, *hispano-americanos*.

The violent break with Spain and Portugal, and the fitful emergence of about fifteen new nations by the 1840s, confronted the leaders of the wars for independence with the need to construct names, symbols, and rituals for the nations and nationalities they sought to create out of the fragments of the collapsing colonial empires. Simón Bolívar, the great liberator of northern South America, dreamed of forging a confederation of the former colonies as one great American nation. Disillusioned, dying, and heading off into exile in late 1830, he could see that his dream had failed, and he concluded that "America is ungovernable" and that "He who serves the revolution ploughs the sea." When he spoke of America, he clearly meant the former Spanish colonies as a whole (and not the United States or Brazil). While most of the new leaders focused on constructing their own nation-states, some intellectuals took Bolívar's larger view and envisioned a region with a common *cultural* identity, if not a political one.

The first documented usage of the term Latin America (in Spanish and French), ironically, emerges in France in the 1850s and 1860s in a series of essays by French, Colombian, and Chilean intellectuals.[2] In part, the term served to contrast Spanish (and sometimes French and Portuguese) America from the growing power of the United States, what these intellectuals called Anglo-Saxon America. Intellectuals and diplomats in the region envisioned a Latin race defined by its cultural heritage of languages (derived from Latin) and religion (Catholicism) opposed to the aggressive and increasingly imperialist, Protestant Anglo-Saxons in the United States. From the French perspective, the effort to stress common cultural bonds between the old Spanish, French, and Portuguese colonies ("Latin" peoples) also served to help justify Napoleon III's imperial ambitions in the Americas, especially his invasion of Mexico in the 1860s. France had also become, by the mid-nineteenth century, the most important cultural influence on the newly ascendant national elites, and that cultural captivation helped to bolster the rationale among intellectuals in the region for adopting the name.

Multiple ironies permeated the creation and then gradual adoption of the name Latin America. First, and most striking, the vast majority of peoples living in the region in the mid-nineteenth century were Native Americans (especially in Mexico, Central America, and the Andes), Afrodescendants (especially in the Caribbean basin and Brazil), and the racially and culturally mixed. In places such as Mexico, Central America, and the Andes, the indigenous majority did not even speak a "Latin" language. Euro-American elites created the Latin modifier as the politically and culturally hegemonic group, but it represented an aspiration, not a reality on the ground. These intellectuals created "Latin" America as a contrast to "Anglo-Saxon" America (the United States), another term that is also deeply ironic. Despite the massive influx of Europeans into North America, even in the 1850s, nearly one in seven inhabitants of the United States was an enslaved person of African descent, native peoples were numerous, and large percentages of the Euro-Americans were neither Anglo-Saxons nor Protestants! As immigration accelerated in the late nineteenth century, the largest waves of immigrants came not from England but from the European continent, especially Southern and Eastern Europe. The misguided creole elites who sought to create Latin American nations had mislabeled *both* their own region and the United States. It was a false and flawed dichotomy from its inception, but one that would have a long life.

As a small but vibrant scholarly community developed in the United States at the beginning of the twentieth century, the term Latin America began to appear in book titles and essays. When this group of scholars created their own journal during the First World War, Latin America remained but one possible term for the region. They debated among themselves and finally settled on the *Hispanic American Historical Review* (not the *Latin American Historical Review*), arguing that the term "Hispanic" also encompassed Portuguese Brazil. It was not until the end of the Second World War that the term Latin America became the most common for the region south of the United States. In the aftermath of the world war and the emergence of the Cold War, for strategic purposes, the U.S. defense and security community divided up the globe. Much of this terminology became standardized in the National Defense Education Act of 1958, a direct response to the perceived threat of the Soviet Union and the launching (in 1957) of Sputnik, the first artificial satellite to circle the Earth. The Act aimed to build up U.S. higher education (especially in math and science) to confront the challenges of the Cold War, especially from the Soviet Union.

The legislation led to the creation of "national resource centers" and "area studies" fellowships funded by the federal government to develop expertise in the various regions of the world. Along with centers for the study of Russia and Eastern Europe, Asia, Africa, and other world regions, the government began funding centers for Latin American studies.[3]

Our current conception of Latin America has its strongest roots in the efforts of foundations and government agencies to "map" world regions in the post-1945 era. The National Research Council, the American Council of Learned Societies, and the Smithsonian Institution formed the Ethnogeographic Board in the 1940s. Through their work, and especially after the passage of the National Defense Education Act, (as with the intelligence and defense communities) academia in the United States carved up the world into regions or areas and universities scrambled to organize "area studies" centers. Latin America, with its seemingly dominant Iberian linguistic, political, and cultural traditions, was one of the most clearly coherent world regions. In many ways, it is a more coherent region than "Europe" or "Southeast Asia," with their multiple languages and ethnicities. In the words of José Moya, the region is "the largest contingent area in the world bound by similar legal practices, language, religion, naming patterns, and the arrangement of urban space."[4] Latin American area studies programs faced dilemmas from their inception in how to deal with "non-Latin" regions and populations, especially in the Caribbean basin (particularly the British West Indies and U.S. territories) and areas that once formed part of the Spanish empire in the Americas, but eventually came under control of the British, the French, the Dutch, and the United States.[5]

The confusion about the boundaries and scope of the region can be seen in the variety of names for Latin American centers in the United States. Some are simply Latin American centers or institutes. Others have been centers for Iberoamerican studies or Latin American and Caribbean studies or centers for Latino and Latin American studies (to include those of Latin American heritage in the United States). At times, some of these centers have been broad enough to be centers for the Americas (as a whole) or transatlantic (Latin American and Iberian studies). Those fifteen or so "national resource centers" receiving government funding are required by law (whatever their name may be) to spend their funds only on "Latin American" programming, that is, not on Latin Americans and their descendants in the U.S. or on the English- or French-speaking Caribbean. The U.S. government very specifically defines the region as the Spanish-speaking nation-states south of the United States (thus excluding Puerto Rico), Brazil, and Haiti.

As government funding and influence shaped the use and definition of Latin America in the United States, the enormous power and presence of the latter, ironically, helped spur a sense of solidarity among the peoples of the region to see themselves as Latin Americans. During the Cold War, Mexicans, Chileans, Brazilians, and the like increasingly spoke of themselves as Latin Americans (*latinoamericanos*) as a means of contrasting themselves with the imperialist power to the north. As with Anglo-Saxons in the nineteenth century, in the postwar struggle Latin Americans often referred to the citizens of the United States as North Americans (*norteamericanos*), another misnomer that should technically include Canadians and Mexicans. Although U.S. citizens like to refer to themselves in English as Americans, the term really encompasses everyone from Arctic Canada to Tierra del Fuego. Understandably, many Latin Americans refuse to use the term and resort to *norteamericanos*, leaving both groups with dubious terminology.

One of the first institutions in the region to apply the terminology was the *Comisión Económica para América Latina* [CEPAL] (Economic Commission for Latin America, or ECLA), created by the United Nations in 1948 and located in Santiago, Chile. Its principal task has been to encourage economic cooperation, especially through the gathering and analysis of data on Latin American economies. In the 1980s, it added the Caribbean to its title (becoming ECLAC and CEPALC). By their count, there are twenty Latin American nations (eighteen Spanish speaking, plus Brazil and Haiti). Over the decades other regional organizations took on the terminology, such as the *Facultad Latinoamericana de Ciencias Sociales* [FLACSO] (Latin American Social Sciences Faculty), created in the 1950s by UNESCO to promote the teaching and influence of the social sciences in the region. Unlike the United States or Europe, Latin American countries rarely have created strong and enduring centers for the study of Latin America or, for that matter, centers for the study of the United States.

As Latin American studies boomed in the 1960s, new professional organizations began to take shape in Europe and the United States, and they adopted the terminology, reinforcing its linguistic dominance. U.S. scholars founded the Latin American Studies Association (LASA) in 1965 along with its own journal, the *Latin American Research Review*. Originally an association primarily for academics in the United States, in the last two decades it has become a truly international organization of more than 12,000 members, two-thirds of them residing outside the United States. Similarly, the Society for Latin American Studies was founded in the United Kingdom in 1964 with its own journal, the *Bulletin of Latin American Research*. The institutional and professional associations, centers, and agencies in the United States, Europe, and Latin America had overwhelmingly adopted the terminology of "Latin America" by the 1970s.

The recent critiques of the term Latin America have roots at least back to the early twentieth century. Intellectuals in regions with indigenous or Afrodescendant majorities in the 1920s and 1930s spoke of Indo America or Afro America. In Mexico and Brazil, the largest countries in the region (and with half the population), intellectuals consciously spurned the Eurocentric visions that had dominated in the nineteenth century and began to emphasize the racially and culturally mixed heritage of Mexicans and Brazilians. They embraced the African and Native American contributions to national culture along with the European (or Latin) heritage. Despite these critiques, the majority of these intellectuals were themselves primarily of European descent, and rarely did they reject the increasingly awkward term Latin America.

The systematic critique of the terminology has taken shape over the last three decades among academics across the Americas and Europe. Much of this discussion has focused on how the terminology emerged among the Europeanized elites in the nineteenth century, together with the role of the

U.S. security and defense communities in promoting it. Walter Mignolo, an Argentine cultural theorist who taught for many years at Duke University, was one of the earliest and most vocal critics, arguing that the terminology was flawed and that Latin America, in fact, did not even exist.[6] The emergence of a powerful wave of identity politics across the Americas has deconstructed the notion of a Latin American identity and has also called into question national identities. Despite regular calls among a wide variety of groups across the Americas for solidarity in the face of the cultural imperialism of the United States, these groups emphasize the multiplicity of identities (especially ethnoracial ones) and de-emphasize national and Latin American identity. The result of the intense conversation about identity over the past three decades has been to leave us in a quandary. Very few would rise today to defend the adequacy of the modifier "Latin" in front of America, yet no one has put forward another label for the region that has gained traction. For the moment, we continue to use this inadequate terminology with an awareness of its limitations, but without a more acceptable name.

Further complicating the conundrum is a lack of consensus on something as seemingly simple as who we should include in the region that we cannot adequately name! A brief survey of the major English-language textbooks on the history of Latin America across the twentieth century quickly reveals the range of definitions. In the U.S., textbooks on Latin America throughout the first half of the twentieth century took a very simple political approach to defining Latin America as the twenty republics that gained their independence in the nineteenth century, from Spain (eighteen countries), Portugal (Brazil), and France (Haiti). (Panama, of course, is an oddity here, having gained its independence as a part of New Granada in the 1820s and then again in 1903 as an "independent" republic. Cuba did not leave the Spanish empire until 1898 and then experienced U.S. occupation until 1902.) From the earliest texts of the founders of the field of Latin American history (such as William Spence Robertson and Percy Alvin Martin, founders of the *Hispanic American Historical Review*) to the journalist Hubert Herring's *A History of Latin America* (1955, 1961, 1968), this was the standard approach. These books were nearly always diplomatic, political, and military history, with only the occasional nod toward society and culture. Even the noted journalist John Gunther, in his wide-ranging travels, did not bother to look beyond the standard twenty republics.[7]

Some of the very first synthetic texts on the region focused solely on Spain in the Americas and went no farther than the colonial period. Charles Edward Chapman, in *Colonial Hispanic America: A History* (1933), includes Brazil, and he rejects the "incorrect term 'Latin America'" in favor of "Hispanic America." The major synthetic surveys in the 1940s and 1950s took as their domain the twenty independent republics. Dana G. Munro, J. Fred Rippy, Donald E. Worcester and Wendell G. Schaeffer all produced encyclopedic surveys. Munro (a former State Department diplomat) covers the colonial period in just over a hundred pages and then takes another 450 to cover the political histories of each of the twenty nations! Much like Herring, Rippy focuses mainly on politics and economics, but with the occasional section on "intellectual life." Worcester and Schaeffer's massive survey (at more than 900 pages) offers a very straightforward political history with little effort to frame the issues or the region. It is classic history as "one damn thing after another." The greatest publishing success of this era is easily John A. Crow's *The Epic of Latin America*, which was first published in 1946. Trained as a scholar of Spanish literature, Crow taught for decades (1937–74) at UCLA. Despite its size (nearly a thousand pages in the last edition), *The Epic of Latin America* has been a huge commercial success, going through four editions over fifty years (1946, 1971, 1980, 1992).[8]

The decolonization of the Caribbean (including here the Guianas) in the 1960s, 1970s, and 1980s clouded the traditional picture, and this can be seen easily in the textbooks published after 1970. One of the biggest selling volumes has been E. Bradford Burns's *Latin America: A Concise Interpretive History*. In the first edition (1972), Burns takes as his subject the "traditional 20," saying that "Geopolitically the region encompasses 18 Spanish-speaking republics, French-speaking Haiti, and Portuguese-speaking Brazil," yet his statistical tables include Barbados, Guyana, Jamaica, and Trinidad and Tobago. By the sixth edition

(1994) this definition has shifted to include "five English-speaking Caribbean nations" (with the Bahamas joining the other four above). Despite the book's title, the statistical tables cover "Latin America and the Caribbean."[9]

Benjamin Keen's *A History of Latin America*, probably the bestselling comprehensive history of Latin America over the last quarter of the twentieth century, covers the "twenty Latin American republics." The very popular recent history of Latin America since independence, John Chasteen's *Born in Blood and Fire*, also takes as its focus the twenty nation-states. What must be the most widely used volume on post-colonial Latin America, Thomas Skidmore and Peter Smith's *Modern Latin America* avoids the thorny problem of definition in its prologue. Yet, the first edition (1984) includes individual chapters on Argentina, Chile, Brazil, Peru, Mexico, Cuba, and Central America (Guatemala, El Salvador, Honduras, Nicaragua, Costa Rica, and Panama). In the second edition (1989), Skidmore and Smith added a chapter on the Caribbean that included Jamaica, Puerto Rico, and the Lesser Antilles, but they do not provide a rationale for their choice of countries. In contrast, Edwin Williamson's *The Penguin History of Latin America* (1992) and Lawrence Clayton and Michael Conniff's *A History of Modern Latin America* (1999) stick to the traditional political definition.[10]

The influential and authoritative *Cambridge History of Latin America* (eleven volumes, 1984–2009) takes Latin America

> to comprise the predominantly Spanish- and Portuguese-speaking areas of continental America south of the United States – Mexico, Central America and South America – together with the Spanish-speaking Caribbean – Cuba, Puerto Rico, the Dominican Republic – and, by convention, Haiti. (The vast territories in North America lost to the United States by treaty and war, first by Spain, then by Mexico, during the first half of the nineteenth century are for the most part excluded. Neither the British, French and Dutch Caribbean islands nor the Guianas are included even though Jamaica and Trinidad, for example, have early Hispanic antecedents ...)[11]

With the exception of Puerto Rico, this definition could easily come from the Munro volume in 1942!

All these definitions hinge on an analysis of some set of common historical processes among nations in the Americas that make them part of something called Latin America, as well as their differences from the United States. With the prominent exception of the traditionalists – and their use of the independent nation-state – very rarely do the authors of histories of Latin America provide an explicit rationale for the areas included in the text. Nevertheless, at the heart of the matter is the notion of what binds these peoples and countries together, a common history that is, at the same time, not shared with the peoples of the United States (or Canada).

At the core of that common history are the processes of invasion, conquest, and colonialism over three centuries, beginning with the "Columbian moment" in 1492. The collision of three peoples – Native Americans, Europeans, and Africans – gave birth to the region we now call Latin America. The moment of conception was the arrival of Columbus and his crew on that warm Caribbean morning in October 1492. Columbus unwittingly brought together two worlds and three peoples, initiating a violent and fertile series of cultural and biological clashes lasting centuries. The histories of the native peoples of the Americas (the New World) and the peoples of Africa and Europe (the Old World) before 1492 took shape in isolation from each other. The history of Latin America begins with the European explorations and invasions and the forced migration of millions of enslaved Africans to the Americas. These conquests and collisions took shape under Spanish and Portuguese colonialism and imperialism. The history of the United States and Canada (and the islands of the Caribbean) is also defined by invasion, conquest, and colonialism. The argument for a common history for what we call Latin America hinges on the belief that Spanish and Portuguese colonialism were similar enough to include Brazil in a region with Spanish America, and different enough from British colonialism to distinguish them from the United States and Canada (and the non-Iberian Caribbean). If one can write and argue for a common history for Latin America, it has its foundations in that colonial heritage of Iberian monarchies subjugating Native Americans and Africans as a labor force to produce agricultural and mining wealth for the European and Euro-American landholding and commercial elites.

With the emergence of transnational studies over the last generation or so, and the increasing importance of migration from Mexico, Central America, and the Caribbean to the United States, the old model of Latin America defined by nation-states has become less viable and harder to defend. What should the historian of Latin America do with the southwestern and southeastern regions of the United States in writing or teaching about the history of Latin America? Are they part of Latin America until the early nineteenth century, and then not after? What about all the Caribbean islands that formed part of the Spanish empire for a century or two before the British, Dutch, and French seized them in the seventeenth and eighteenth centuries? Even more complicated, what about Puerto Rico? By all indicators (history, language, culture), Puerto Rico is Latin American, but it is politically part of the United States (the only "free associated state"). As millions of immigrants from south of its current political border have flowed into the United States in the last fifty years, the longstanding cultural and historical ties across both sides of the border have been reinforced. The second largest urban population of Salvadorans, for example, is in Los Angeles. The concentration of Mexican immigrants in several major U.S. cities makes them some of the largest Mexican cities, but outside of Mexico. In short, using the political, nation-state definition of Latin America excludes large sections of North America that are culturally and linguistically Latin American.

The history of the region since independence in the early nineteenth century has been one of increasing diversity and divergence. As each of the nation-states, territories, and adjacent regions has taken its own historical path, they have each reshaped, transformed, and discarded more and more of their common colonial heritage. That shared past of conquest, colonization, and Iberian control recedes into the past after two centuries of separation from the European metropolis. Guatemala, for example, has less and less in common with, say, Argentina and Brazil. Cuba and Bolivia become increasingly distinct and distant from their shared history. In short, even if we can argue (and I believe we can) that what makes Latin America a coherent region is a common history over several centuries, the shared heritage forged in that colonial past is less and less central to their present circumstances. The cultural, economic, and political processes and patterns that once defined the region have increasingly diverged over the past two centuries. In 2092, on the six-hundredth anniversary of the controversial and transformative Columbian voyage, we may find it very difficult to define Latin America as a coherent world region, either with the term Latin America or with some other name we may eventually create.

2
The Pioneering Generations

History and Colonialism

The "diary" of the much celebrated, much maligned Christopher Columbus is the origin text on the collision of cultures that began in 1492. Columbus kept a daily logbook during the seven months of his momentous transatlantic voyage. Although the original has been lost, the Dominican priest and chronicler of the conquest, Bartolomé de las Casas, transcribed and summarized the document in his *Historia de las Indias*, composed in the mid-sixteenth century.[1] The earliest historical accounts of what we now call Latin America came from the writings of colonial officials (especially priests like Las Casas), conquistadors (such as Columbus or Cortés), and (in rarer cases) the indigenous peoples of the region (particularly in Mexico and Central America). The Spanish and Portuguese conquests generated a series of historical works, often by participants anxious to highlight their own exploits in the eyes of the monarchy and royal officials. The conquest of Mexico and Central America spawned detailed and rich narratives by Spaniards and Native Americans alike. The letters of Hernán Cortés to Emperor Charles V and the Aztec versions of the conquest are vivid examples of some of the earliest historical accounts of the birth of this region we call Latin America.[2]

Throughout the colonial period (roughly 1490s to 1820s), these historical accounts appeared in print, while some remained hidden in archives and libraries only to come to light in later centuries. The accounts in Spanish and Portuguese during the three centuries of colonial rule generally referred to the region as the Indies, the New World, or America. At times, accounts referred to Spanish America or Portuguese America. Although Spain created universities in Santo Domingo, Mexico City, and Lima as early as the mid-sixteenth century, universities consisted mainly of faculties for the study of law, medicine, and engineering. In Brazil, the monarchy did not even create faculties of medicine, law, and engineering until the first decades of the nineteenth century! The modern liberal arts college with history departments would not appear until the twentieth century in most of the region. In the United States and Europe, it would be the late nineteenth century before any historian based in a university published books on the history of Latin America.

Nineteenth-Century Origins

Until the emergence of the first professional academic historians in the late nineteenth century, men of independent wealth and means in the United States, Europe, and Latin America, "gentlemen scholars," produced the first serious scholarship on the history of Latin America. Across the Atlantic world, romanticism dominated elite culture and historical writing in the first half of the nineteenth century, and positivism the second half. Romanticism emphasized the power of nature, the heroic individual, and the so-called spirit of the people (*Zeitgeist* in German). Positivism glorified the scientific method and led to an emphasis on facts, documents, and "how things actually were" (*wie es eigentlich gewesen*, in the famous words of the German historian Leopold von Ranke). Service in the United States diplomatic corps in Spain spurred Washington Irving (1783–1859) to write the immensely popular and influential *A History of the Life and Voyages of Christopher Columbus* (1828). Perhaps the greatest work of the nineteenth century was William Hickling

Prescott's *History of the Conquest of Mexico* (1843), an epic account that remains in print to the present. Although Irving and Prescott (1796–1859) admired the heroic exploits of Columbus and Cortés and saw them as representing the forces of "civilization" against the "barbarism" of the Native Americans, their writings also contained a strong Anglo-American and Protestant bias. As Benjamin Keen observed, they viewed the "Spaniards as a people with a romantic past, but backward and priest-ridden."[3]

In the second half of the nineteenth century, the romanticism of Irving and Prescott gave way to the positivism and social evolutionism of scholars who had taken an interest in Latin American history often after embarking on successful business careers. Under the influence of Darwin's theory of evolution in the natural world, intellectuals such as Herbert Spencer (1820–1903) theorized that all peoples and societies evolved, and that the more "complex" societies were not only more "sophisticated" but also morally superior. Lewis Henry Morgan (1818–1881) and his disciple Adolph Bandelier (1840–1914) became founding figures in the emergence of modern anthropology with their studies of Native American indigenous societies. Bandelier produced monumental works on Mesoamerican societies, in particular, the Aztecs. Both considered even the highly complex Native American cultures of Mesoamerica to be barbaric and "low" on the ladder of human social evolution. Charles F. Lummis (1859–1928), a popular writer, helped make Bandelier's work and views more widely known through his book *The Spanish Pioneers* (1893), which went through seven editions by 1917.

Perhaps the most important historian of the era in the United States was Hubert Howe Bancroft (1832–1918) who used his personal fortune to accumulate a vast library and archive on the western United States, Mexico, and Central America. (His collection became the basis of the Latin American library at the University of California, Berkeley, and bears his name today.) Using teams of research assistants to copy and purchase documents, Bancroft's "factory system" churned out the monumental *History of the Pacific States* between 1874 and 1890. (The first six volumes cover the "native races," the next three, Central America, and the last six, Mexico.)

In Britain, the Scottish minister and head of the University of Edinburgh, William Robertson (1721–1793), produced a massive *History of America* (1777). Despite its title, the three volumes synthesize the history of Spanish America, and, much like Prescott and Bancroft in their works, Robertson writes with a condescension toward native peoples and Catholicism. The English Romantic poet Robert Southey (1774–1843) became enamored of Portugal and its empire and penned a three-volume *History of Brazil* (1810–19). Even more so than in the United States, the appearance of academic historians writing about Latin America lagged, well into the twentieth century. In Spain and Portugal, the emphasis of historians, not surprisingly, was on the empire, and the American colonies formed a part of the larger story.

The wars for independence consumed much of the 1810s and 1820s in Latin America, and the new nations that emerged had to create their own rituals, symbols, and myths – in the words of Benedict Anderson, their own "imagined communities." Some of the major intellectual figures who produced the new national histories were also prominent political figures. Two major political figures, Lucas Alamán (1792–1853) in Mexico and Bartolomé Mitre (1821–1906) in Argentina, penned classic historical works that influenced generations who followed them. As in the United States, romanticism defined the histories written before 1870. In the later decades of the century French and German influence continued, and an emphasis on the collection of documents and research led to increasingly sophisticated works. Notable examples are the works of Joaquín García Icazbalceta (*Bibliografía mexicana del siglo XVI*, 1886) and Vicente Riva Palacio (*México a través de los siglos*, 5 vols, 1885–9) in Mexico; Diego Barros Arana (*Historia general de Chile*, 16 vols, 1884–1902) in Chile; Gabriel René Moreno (*Últimos días coloniales en el Alto Perú*, 1896) in Bolivia; and Sebastián Lorente (*Historia de la civilización peruana*, 1879) in Peru.

Throughout the nineteenth century, gentlemen scholars created a series of institutes and societies to support their research, writing, and collegiality. National academies or societies of history (and often geography) took shape as early as the 1830s, but most came together in the later decades of the century. At the same time, these new nations organized (and reorganized) national and provincial archives and published collections of documents, especially those associated with the struggles for independence or with the colonial foundations of the emerging nation-states. Nearly all these efforts served to produce a narrative and documentary support to justify the nation's existence and, at times, its inevitability. The Mexicans quickly found in their Aztec past a classical era improved upon by three centuries of European rule and now brought to fruition with independence and national sovereignty. The Brazilians (and others) also turned to their indigenous past as central to the nation's creation under the guidance of the Iberian colonizers. Although conquered, killed, or driven off their lands in much of the Americas, the "noble savage" became a powerful symbol of national identity in many American nations in the nineteenth century.[4]

Professionalization: An Academic Community Emerges (on Three Continents)

By the 1880s, especially under the influence of German universities and scholars, the historical profession in the United States had begun to emerge. Ranke's vision of history – collecting and organizing documents, recounting "how things actually were," training graduate students in a seminar setting, and producing the scholarly monograph – increasingly defined the profession in the last decades of the nineteenth century and the first decades of the twentieth. One important sign of this professionalization was the founding of the American Historical Association in 1884. The first academic historians of Latin America in the United States were Bernard Moses (1846–1930) and Edward Gaylord Bourne (1860–1908). According to Benjamin Keen, Moses was "the first professor of Latin American history in the United States and the first to write monographs of the modern type on colonial Latin America."[5] Trained in Germany, Moses produced a series of books from the 1890s through the 1920s while on the faculty of the University of California, Berkeley. Bourne, who taught at Yale University, published the influential

Spain in America (1904). Both Moses' and Bourne's works were shaped by the Social Darwinism and the colonialism of the era. Building on the works of Prescott and Bancroft, these authors viewed Catholicism and racial mixture as key reasons for Latin America's "backwardness." Like their predecessors, they generally viewed Spain's colonial enterprise as beneficial for Latin America bringing civilization to the New World. The parallels between United States colonial expansion after 1898 and the Spanish imperial experience were ever present in their writings, and both took a direct interest in the Philippines (another former Spanish colony recently seized by the United States).[6]

Bourne and many others were revisionists who consciously sought to reject or move away from the nineteenth-century emphasis on the so-called Black Legend propagated by Protestants in England and the Netherlands beginning in the sixteenth century – i.e. that the Spanish had systematically annihilated native populations through a cruel and ferocious conquest in the sixteenth century. One of the most influential of these works was *The Encomienda in New Spain* (1929) by Lesley Byrd Simpson, a scholar at Berkeley. As Keen astutely pointed out, Simpson and other revisionists adopted "a relativism that shunned moral judgments (though not consistently), a pragmatic, 'hard-boiled' approach that viewed colonial conquest and exploitation as unfortunate, but inevitable, facts of life, and a tendency to assess Spanish colonial policy from the standpoint of Spanish rather than Indian interests." They lacked an anthropological perspective.[7] The revisionist approach continued well into the 1950s.

Along with studies of the colonial period, diplomatic and political history dominated the field well into the 1940s. The emergence of the United States as a world power, especially in the Caribbean basin after 1898, paralleled and intertwined with the professionalization of Latin American history in the United States. William Spence Robertson, Dexter Perkins, and Arthur P. Whitaker were pioneer figures in writing the history of United States–Latin American relations. In the years after the First World War, much of this diplomatic history came from a "liberal internationalist" perspective that stressed the need for a strong U.S. guiding presence in the region as the leader in the "Pan American" movement.[8]

A sign of the growing professionalization of the field was the founding of the *Hispanic American Historical Review* during the First World War. Charles E. Chapman, who taught at the University of California at Berkeley, and William Spence Robertson, of the University of Illinois, conceived of the idea of a separate journal of Latin American history while at a conference in Buenos Aires in 1916. After soliciting funds and assistance from colleagues in academia and the business world over the next two years, they began publication of the journal in 1918. (Financial problems forced the suspension of publication between 1922 and 1926.) Early circulation hovered around 500 copies. The journal remains the most prestigious in the field of Latin American history in the United States.

By the mid-1920s, a group of historians had begun to hold their own luncheon and sessions at the annual meeting of the American Historical Association, calling themselves the "Hispanic American History group." In 1928, they created the Conference on Hispanic American History, an organization formally reorganized and reconstituted in 1937 at the American Historical Association meeting in Philadelphia as the Conference on Latin-American History. (They later dropped the hyphen.) Chapman and Robertson were key figures along with a growing group of academic colleagues. During the 1930s, scholars from a variety of disciplines, with the assistance of the Social Science Research Council, started the *Handbook of Latin American Studies*, which eighty years later remains one of the central bibliographical tools for researchers.

The emergence of professional academic history was more complex and varied in Latin America given its diversity and size. In places such as Argentina and Chile, the universities developed quickly in the nineteenth and twentieth centuries, and historians with academic affiliations appeared sooner than in places such as Brazil or Central America. In Mexico, the reign of Porfirio Díaz (1876–1911) and then the Mexican Revolution (1910–20) stimulated the production of historical works. During the Porfiriato, many of these works served to justify the ruler's nation-building project. In the aftermath of the revolution, a new regime and powerful support for cultural institutions forged a new vision of

Mexico emphasizing the indigenous past and racial mixture (*mestizaje*) as the defining feature of national history and identity. The investment in education and culture in Chile, Argentina, and Mexico would be crucial to professionalizing the historical profession and academic history by the Second World War. In Brazil, the late start for universities (1930s and 1940s) left the field of history to intellectuals and writers well into the mid-twentieth century. The defining historical works in Brazil in the early twentieth century were all written by independent intellectuals: Euclídes da Cunha's *Rebellion in the Backlands* (*Os sertões*, 1902), Gilberto Freyre's *Masters and the Slaves* (*Casa-grande e senzala*, 1933), Sérgio Buarque de Holanda's *Roots of Brazil* (*Raízes do Brasil*, 1936), and Caio Prado Júnior's *The Colonial Background of Modern Brazil* (*Formação do Brasil contemporâneo*, 1942).

In the United States, the professionalization of the field resulted, in part, from the emergence of dynamic and productive scholars whose works attracted attention within the historical profession in general, and whose students went on to spread the teaching of Latin American history at universities across the country. Two figures deserve to be singled out. Clarence H. Haring (1885–1960), a Rhodes Scholar and a Harvard Ph.D. (1916), began teaching Latin American history at Harvard while a graduate student. His early work focused on trade, navigation, and buccaneers, and he turned to Latin America in the early 1920s. Haring's *The Spanish Empire in America* (1947) is a classic example of the work of the pre-boom years concentrating on politics, institutions, and archival research in Seville. He taught at Yale (1916–23) and then at Harvard (1923–53) and remained active in the profession until his death in 1960. The other notable pioneer professional is Herbert Eugene Bolton (1870–1953).

No other figure looms as large in the field of Latin American history in the United States as Bolton. Like many of the early academic historians of Latin America, Bolton did not do his graduate work in Latin American history. Trained at the University of Pennsylvania (Ph.D., 1899) he went to the University of Texas in 1901 to teach medieval and European history. Almost immediately, he was drawn to the history of Spanish colonization in Texas through his interest in Catholic priests and missionaries. In 1902, he made his first venture into the archives of Mexico, the first of many trips, eventually leading to the publication of the *Guide to Materials for the History of the United States in the Principal Archives of Mexico* (1913).

These early years in Texas guided Bolton firmly in the direction of the history of the "borderlands," those areas of the United States – principally the southwestern and southeastern states – once part of the Spanish empire in North America. Bolton's career, and the many students he trained, straddled two once distinct fields, the history of the United States and the history of Latin America. Bolton's history is that of the archival historian, closely tied to documents and their explication. First, and foremost, he wrote narrative history in the heroic and romantic nineteenth-century tradition, the tale of explorers, missionaries, and conquistadors with little direct interest in Native American cultures. Bolton was a hispanophile in the tradition of Prescott and Bancroft.

After moving to Stanford University in 1909 and then Berkeley in 1911, Bolton embarked upon a prolific career producing many books and students. Between 1914 and 1944 he directed more than 100 doctoral dissertations, including those of some of the major figures in the field from the 1920s well into the last years of the century (Charles E. Chapman, Herbert I. Priestley, Charles W. Hackett, J. Fred Rippy, John Lloyd Mecham, John Tate Lanning, Irving A. Leonard, Woodrow Borah, and William J. Griffith, to name a few). In the 1950s, after his death, all three Latin American historians at Berkeley were his former students. The golden age of "Boltonians," however, was the 1920s to the 1960s, as Bolton's students spread out across the United States creating programs in borderlands history (usually with an emphasis on the United States) and in Latin American history.

Bolton asserted his most famous – and controversial – contribution to the field in his presidential address to the American Historical Association in Toronto in 1932. He argued for an end to the separation of United States, Canadian, and Latin American history into separate and self-contained fields. Instead, he emphasized the common "history of the Americas" – colonization by European powers, colonial exploitation, wars for independence, transatlantic migration. Putting his ideas into practice, he long taught a huge lecture course at Berkeley, "History of the Americas," that presented the "epic of greater America" as a single course and set of processes. Bolton's emphasis on working in foreign archives and his stress on larger, common processes were major contributions to the development of the field in the United States. Through his training of several generations of historians, he did more than any other figure in the twentieth century to expand and professionalize Latin American history in the United States. As the decades passed, however, few took up his call to study the history of all the Americas. Most of his students, and their students, eventually identified themselves as specialists in United States or Latin American history.

On the Eve of the Boom

In the 1940s and 1950s an academic community of perhaps a few hundred scholars and non-academics began to produce a growing literature of high quality and rigor in Latin America, Europe, and the United States. In Europe, this was a very small group, with the most prominent figures in Spain, Portugal, France, and the United Kingdom. The growth of academic history programs in Latin America was most notable in Mexico, Argentina, and Chile. In the United States, the steady growth of the postwar economy, universities, and enrollments consolidated the field, especially around a series of prominent scholars at about a dozen universities. There were some parallels with the development of the profession in the United States, but also some significant differences. The influence of Leopold von Ranke's emphasis on archival research and documentary evidence formed the basis of historical methodology on both sides of the Atlantic. French influence, especially of the Annales School, had enormous impact across Latin America and Europe, but less so in the United States. Broadly interpretative works, theory, and the essayistic tradition had much greater sway in Latin America than in the English-language literature.

The influence of Ranke was pronounced in Latin America, although with wide variations across the region. In the aftermath of the Mexican Revolution, what would become the governing party in Mexico for the rest of the century, the Institutional Revolutionary Party (*Partido Revolucionario Institucional*, or PRI), actively sought to construct a new narrative of national identity. The regime put into place a variety of educational and cultural institutions – schools, museums, institutes – to produce a new vision, a new history of Mexico. As in Brazil (and a number of other countries), narratives of national identity turned away from the Eurocentrism of the Iberian empires and toward racial and cultural mixture. The new narrative of national identity glorified the indigenous (especially Aztec) past, the mixing of races (*mestizaje*) over centuries, and the revolution as the triumph of a modern, secular, *mestizo* Mexico. By the 1960s, Mexico had a vibrant and productive community of professional historians teaching, researching, and producing sophisticated historical works. Ironically, a desire to explain the Mexican Revolution, and its perceived "betrayal" by the 1950s, motivated many of these historians (and social scientists).

An additional impetus in Mexico was the arrival of Spanish intellectuals fleeing the fascist regime of Francisco Franco beginning in the late 1930s. Rafael Altamira (1866–1951) and José Gaos (1900–1969) – to name but two examples – contributed greatly to the intellectual and professional development of the humanities and social sciences. The founding of the Colegio de México in 1940 is emblematic of the era, as it became a leading intellectual force and crucial to the consolidation of academic history. Silvio Zavala and Daniel Cosío Villegas are perhaps the two iconic figures of the era. Zavala (1909–2014) assumed increasingly powerful administrative roles in the major historical institutions (Colegio de México, Museo Nacional de Historia, Historical Commission of the Panamerican Institute of History and Geography), becoming "almost a 'Tsar' of history."[9] Cosío Villegas (1898–1976) began a long-running research seminar at the Colegio de México in the late 1940s that trained many professional historians and exerted an enormous influence on the historiography. He edited the *Historia moderna de México* (1955–72), an enormously collaborative work in ten volumes that established a style of history in the Rankean tradition emphasizing archival research and documentation. Cosío Villegas also founded (with support from the government) the Fondo de Cultura Económica, which became one of the most important publishers of academic works in the humanities and social sciences, not only in Mexico but throughout Latin America.

In those nations that invested early and in a sustained fashion in education (most notably, Argentina, Chile, Uruguay) universities began to develop graduate programs in history. By the 1950s, Argentine historians had split into contending schools with differing visions of the country's national narrative, but both employed sophisticated methods to make their claims. Perhaps the most influential work in these years was José Luis Romero's *Las ideas políticas en la Argentina* (1946). Romero (1909–1977) would play a prominent role in universities and the diffusion of social history, French historical methods, and German philosophy in Argentine (and Latin American) history.[10]

With the works produced from the beginnings of the conquest to independence, the history of Latin America begins in Spain and Portugal as the history of colonies and empire. The professionalization of the history of Latin America in both countries, however, lags behind the Americas, as well as in Britain and France. By and large, the historical works produced in both countries has been dominated by an imperial gaze, the metropolis looking outwards at the empire. The prolific Portuguese historian Vitorino Magalhães Godinho (1918–2011) published many important volumes on the empire deeply influenced by the methods of the Annales School. He spent much of the 1960s and early 1970s working in French institutions. In both countries, dictatorships in the twentieth century (Antonio de Oliveira Salazar in Portugal and Francisco Franco in Spain) constrained the development of the profession. Nonetheless, the rich archives in Spain and Portugal became meccas for historians of the colonial era in Latin America. Given these riches so close to home, historians in Spain and Portugal (as well as France) have tended to concentrate their work on the centuries before independence.

The emergence of an early academic community in France, especially in Paris, took shape with the rise of the Annales

School. Taking its name from their famous academic journal (*Annales d'histoire économique et sociale*, founded 1929), historians such as Marc Bloch and Lucien Febvre largely studied the medieval and early modern world, but their disciples, especially in Latin America, also emphasized structures, quantitative data, and the *longue durée* (long term). This influence would be especially pronounced in Latin America in the post-1945 decades. The longstanding fascination of Latin American elites with Paris and French culture translated into pronounced French influence in Latin American universities in the twentieth century. The classic early academic works in France (as in Spain and Portugal) tend to be imperial in perspective, often emphasizing quantitative and social history.

In Great Britain, the field took some time to emerge but blossomed in the 1960s. Although Britain had been the dominant power in most of Latin America and parts of the Caribbean from the early nineteenth century until the Second World War, historians in the United Kingdom virtually ignored the region until the 1960s, with a few notable exceptions. The "founding figure" in Britain was Robin Humphreys (1907–1999), originally trained as a historian of North America. Appointed to the first chair in Latin American history in the U.K., in 1948, he worked in "profound intellectual isolation."[11] The graduate students of the 1950s, John Lynch (1927–2018) and J. H. Elliott (b. 1930), among others, would become the notable young historians of the 1960s (along with David Joslin, Alistair Hennessy, Harold Blakemore, and John Street). Charles Boxer (1904–2000) was to become one of the foremost historians of colonial Brazil, but through a rather circuitous and unique route. A British naval officer in Japan and China in the 1930s and 1940s, Boxer began his career publishing on the Portuguese empire in East Asia, became the first Camões Chair of Portuguese at Kings College London in 1947, and went on to write many works on the Portuguese, Spanish, and Dutch "seaborne" empires. His *Golden Age of Brazil, 1695–1750* (1963) remains a classic.[12]

Although Bolton and his students trained ever larger numbers of historians as specialists in Latin American history, some of the major figures of this generation were trained more broadly in the history of Western civilization. They approached Latin America as a part of the process of the global expansion of European civilization. The great figures of this generation, in time, became the senior scholars who witnessed the boom in Latin American history after 1959. Born around the time of the First World War or shortly thereafter, this generation did their graduate work in the late 1940s and early 1950s. They were generally in their late thirties or early forties when the boom began.

Alexander Marchant and Richard Morse are prime examples of some of the last historians of Latin America trained not as specialists, but as generalists. Marchant (1912–1981), born in Rio de Janeiro in a family of Confederate expatriates (*confederados*), did his doctoral work at Johns Hopkins University in the 1930s under the guidance of Frederic Chapin Lane, an eminent historian of European overseas expansion. Marchant chose as his dissertation topic the Portuguese settlement of Brazil because it was a poorly studied part of the process of the "expansion overseas of the peoples of Europe in the sixteenth century." When his dissertation appeared as a book in 1942, it was only the second academic monograph on Brazilian history published in the United States, a sure sign of how historical studies of Brazil lagged far behind work on Spanish America.[13]

Richard Morse (1922–2001), another Brazilianist, also trained broadly in the history of the West, especially intellectual history. Morse, more so than any other figure in the field, carried the banner of cultural and intellectual history. Although it has a long and venerable tradition, the intellectual history of Latin America in the United States has never been at the forefront of the discipline. The works of John Tate Lanning on the Enlightenment in Latin America and Lewis Hanke on Bartolomé de las Casas are examples of the kind of traditional intellectual history done in the 1940s and 1950s. Morse, something of an intellectual gadfly, wrote prolifically in an essayist style. He emphasized the patrimonial, Catholic heritage of the region, contrasting it with the individualistic Protestant heritage of North America.[14]

One of the clearest shifts in the field after 1940 was an increasing interest in the post-colonial period and national level studies. The early generations of academic historians were overwhelmingly interested in the colonial era, concentrating on the era of the conquest (roughly the 1490s to the 1570s in Mexico and the Andes) and the decades just before and after independence (roughly 1750–1850). Most of the studies of the post-colonial period written in the first few decades of the twentieth century took a decidedly diplomatic and political approach. As late as 1930, Percy Alvin Martin of Stanford University flatly stated that "the Hispanic American republics have no history worthy of the name," and that "the task of the historian ... is finished when he has adequately investigated the colonial period and the wars of independence."[15]

Understandably, Mexico led the way in studies of the national period; in particular, United States scholars had a keen interest in the Mexican Revolution. Frank Tannenbaum, a sociologist at Columbia University, Howard Cline, Stanley Ross, and Charles Cumberland produced important works on the revolution and United States–Mexican relations.[16] In the decades since, scholarship on Mexican history has been far and away the most developed for all the Latin American nations. (Studies of the Mexican Revolution in English alone dwarf the literature produced in English on countries such as Uruguay, Paraguay, Ecuador or Costa Rica.)[17]

Other notable shifts in the 1940s and 1950s were the move toward more social and economic history and the influence of other disciplines on the field. Perhaps the most influential approach came to be known as the "Berkeley School," with its emphasis on demographic history. Woodrow Borah (a Bolton Ph.D., 1940), Lesley Byrd Simpson, and Sherburne F. Cook teamed up to produce a series of important studies on the indigenous populations of central Mexico in the sixteenth century.[18] Borah and Cook's meticulous archival research documented a demographic catastrophe in central Mexico in the aftermath of the conquest, with indigenous populations declining by as much as 80 to 90 percent. Subsequent studies over the last half century have generally upheld their pioneering work and extended it to other regions of the Americas.

The Berkeley School helped open the field to the influences from demography, anthropology, and other social sciences. Charles Gibson (1920–1985), who did his graduate work at

Yale in the late 1940s, also pushed the field in the direction of ethnohistory. His monumental *The Aztecs under Spanish Rule* (1964) influenced dozens of scholars in history and anthropology in the boom generation.[19] Along with that of the Berkeley School, Gibson's pioneering work helped turn historians of the colonial period from their earlier concentration on the conquerors to a discovery of the indigenous peoples and their history. Despite his focus on Indians, Gibson still relied on Spanish-language documents to get at the world of the Aztecs and their contemporaries.

This generation also helped move social and economic history increasingly to the forefront of the field. Perhaps the most influential figure in this era was Stanley Stein (1920–2019), a Harvard Ph.D. (1951) who worked with Clarence Haring. In 1957, Stein published two fundamental books on Brazilian economic history (both rural and urban), *The Brazilian Cotton Manufacture* and *Vassouras: A Brazilian Coffee County, 1850–1900*. The latter, in particular, exerted enormous influence on scholars of slavery. Much like Gibson's Mexico, Stein's Brazil took shape out of the notarial archives of municipalities, bringing to light in greater detail than ever before the lives not only of the elites but also of other social classes.

In many ways, the most influential historian of this generation was Howard F. Cline (1915–1971), another Harvard Ph.D. (1947). Cline was perhaps the prime organizer and promoter of the field in the United States in the 1950s and 1960s. As director of the Hispanic Foundation at the Library of Congress, he spearheaded some of the most important projects in the field, including the *National Directory of Latin Americanists* and the two-volume compilation *Latin American History: Essays on Its Study and Teaching, 1898–1965*.[20] Cline was also a key figure in mobilizing government and foundation funds to support Latin American studies in the United States.

As Cline's directory documents, by the end of the 1950s a small, but vibrant and productive, group of historians of Latin America had taken shape in the United States. In Europe, an even smaller community had emerged. Across Latin America, some universities had begun to produce excellent academic history and historians, prominently in Mexico and

Argentina. Midway through the twentieth century, many decades of slow and gradual development had put into place communities of historians of Latin America on three continents. Little did they suspect that the field of Latin American history would be transformed profoundly in the 1960s by a convergence of historical events and processes.

3
The Economic and Quantitative Turns

El Boom

A number of factors converged to produce a boom in Latin American studies after 1960. Area studies programs, in general, began to take off in the 1950s as a direct consequence of the Cold War. Both the United States government and private foundations provided growing funding to train specialists in the various regions of the world in an era of United States globalism. The National Defense Education Act (1958) provided funding to create a pool of experts in all areas of the globe. The Ford Foundation, to take one example, doled out more than $270 million to thirty-four universities between 1953 and 1966 in its International Training and Research Program.[1] Another vital factor was the rapid growth of the number of students entering universities in the 1960s, the postwar "baby boomers" reaching college age. (University enrollments rose by more than 100 percent from 1960 to 1970.) Established universities rapidly added to their faculties, new universities came into existence, and all broadened their history departments beyond the traditional "core" fields of United States and European history. The demand for trained specialists increased and the number of graduate students entering Latin American history programs escalated.

Finally, one cannot overlook the impact of Fidel Castro and the Cuban Revolution. Castro clearly captured the attention of the United States government and public and helped spur the demand for Latin American specialists, including historians. The revolutionary upheavals across Latin America in the 1960s further spurred many a student to choose Latin America as his or her field of study. In the 1960s, a significant number of entering graduate students had experience in Latin America through the Peace Corps or volunteer work. Probably more so than in most fields, historians of Latin America often were drawn to the field by direct experience in the region or a strong concern for issues of social justice and equity. The translation of major works, especially novels, into English dramatically raised awareness of the brilliance of Latin American literature after 1960 and even led to the coining of the term "el boom" to describe its florescence and global influence.

Expansion, diversification, and specialization characterize the field after 1960. The enormous and rapid growth of historians of Latin America in United States universities fundamentally transformed the profession, especially after the graduate students of the 1960s became the professors of the 1970s. The number of dissertations, for example, on Latin American history grew from about a dozen in 1960 to four times that by 1980. An expanding United States economy and growing numbers of foundations and agencies (Ford, Rockefeller, Doherty, Tinker, United States Department of Health, Education, and Welfare, the Social Science Research Council, for example) quickly opened up travel and archival research in Latin America for United States graduate students and professors on an unprecedented scale. By the early 1970s, scholars were working on all types of topics – political, economic, social, cultural, intellectual, diplomatic. Like many in the historical profession, historians of Latin America would turn to innovative new approaches, but the next generation of scholarship would be primarily in social and economic history.

The 1960s mark the great watershed in the professionalization and growth of Latin American history – in the United States, Europe, and Latin America. Economic growth, rising university enrollments, and revolutionary upheaval spurred the formation of academic communities on three continents (with much, much smaller groups in Australia and Asia). The boom in Latin American studies decelerated with the global economic downturn in 1973–4, provoked by the first oil crisis, a slowdown then reinforced by the second oil crisis in 1979–80. These global economic shocks slowed the formation of professional historians from the mid-1970s to the mid-1980s. When the world economy began slowly to recover in the mid-1980s, the pipeline of academic historians stabilized in the United States and the United Kingdom at a small, but steady, stream. The massive decade of debt crisis in Latin America that would last into the early 1990s, ironically, marked the beginnings of a decades-long expansion of doctoral programs in Latin American universities. Accelerating in the early 2000s, this trend marked the consolidation of a professional academic community of historians of Latin America – in the Americas and Europe. The 1970s and 1980s, then, are transitional decades. The consolidation of the field, despite tough global economic conditions, took shape in the decades just before the transportation and digital revolutions would finally make it possible to connect historians of Latin America, regardless of location, in the early twenty-first century.

Since the 1970s, Latin American history has truly come of age as a field of specialization in the United States. The proliferation of scholars studying all periods as well as all the countries of the region has intensified over the past four decades. Historians of Latin America in the United States now pursue a wide array of historical approaches with increasing specialization. The cross-fertilization that began in the 1960s with the social sciences has continued, as does the influence of other fields of history and the humanities. Although the boom transformed the profession, the seemingly limitless job opportunities for new historians in the late 1960s turned into a nightmarish dearth of employment opportunities by the mid-1970s. By 1975, U.S. universities annually produced more than 1,000 new doctorates (in all fields of history), with just half that number of jobs available in academic departments. The field of Latin American history, as the profession in general, trained many promising young scholars who subsequently went on to careers in other professions in the late 1970s and early 1980s. Many a dissertation became the endpoint in an academic career, rather than the start, and never reached publication.[2]

By the mid-1980s, however, the glut of new doctorates had eased, and the job market revived (although with nowhere near the dynamism of the booming 1960s). By the 1990s, the number of new doctorates in Latin American history each year continued to exceed the number of academic job openings. United States and European history accounted for about 70 percent of all doctorates in history in the last decade of the twentieth century. Latin American history accounted for around 5 to 6 percent. This translated into around fifty to sixty new doctorates each year, with about forty to fifty jobs advertised as Latin American history positions. Many of the new Ph.D.s were women, a sign of the changing times in academia as the number of women entering graduate school in history and receiving their doctorates rose steadily.[3]

The size, diversity, and fragmentation of the field make it impossible to generalize as readily as for earlier decades. Some clear trends do stand out. Most notably, the 1970s and 1980s were the decades of social history, just as cultural history dominates after 1990. Continuing a major shift that had begun in the 1960s, social historians turned their attention away from institutions and elites to collective mentalities and non-elites, such as the enslaved, indigenous peoples, women, workers, and peasants. Social historians did not abandon the study of elites but often now studied them as collective entities seeking patterns and group or class identity. The decline of more traditional historical approaches – political, diplomatic, military – continued in the closing decades of the century.

The Quantitative "Moment"

Along with the turn to social history after 1960, Latin American history experienced a "quantitative moment," accompanied by the rest of the historical profession (and some of the social sciences). Seemingly, historians began to count everything – people, goods, trade, prices. Quantification was not an entirely new phenomenon. Earl J. Hamilton's classic *American Treasure and the Price Revolution in Spain, 1501–1650* (1934) was one of the earliest scholarly monographs on Latin American history and a pioneering work in economic history in general. Reconstructing the flows of silver from Mexico and Peru to Spain, Hamilton showed a small but important rise in prices over decades, an inflationary phenomenon that demonstrated the crucial linkage between American silver and Europe's economy. Stanley Stein's work on cotton manufacturing in Brazil and his book on slavery and coffee (both published in 1957) made important use of statistics and data gathering.

The Berkeley School is also an early example of quantitative history in the United States. Woodrow Borah (1912–1999), Sherburne Cook (1896–1974), and Lesley Byrd Simpson (1891–1984) began studying the demography of central Mexico in the 1940s, and their work would become the standard for estimating native populations in the Americas (pre- and post-conquest) in the succeeding decades. (Incredibly, none of them was in the History Department. Cook was a physiologist and Simpson in the Spanish Department. Borah was in the Speech Department until the early 1960s, when he took an endowed chair in the History Department.) This demographic work attracted a vibrant group of researchers in the following decades, in a variety of disciplines. Henry Dobyns (1925–2009), an anthropologist, published key work in the 1960s and 1970s, especially on Peru. Noble David Cook (b. 1941) also produced exceptionally rigorous demographic work on colonial Peru, while Robert McCaa (b. 1942) applied highly sophisticated statistical analysis to data on Chile and Peru. Linda Newson (b. 1946), a British geographer, contributed to this longstanding discussion about the collapse of pre-Columbian indigenous populations after 1492 with her work, beginning in the 1980s, on Central America and Ecuador.[4]

By the 1970s, the quantitative turn ranged from scholars who regularly constructed tables and graphs to those who argued that, ultimately, quantification was the only truly empirically rigorous and valid form of historical knowledge production. Proponents of quantification often referred to the application of quantification to history as cliometrics (after the muse of history, Clio). Perhaps the epitome of the move toward quantification was Robert Fogel and Stanley Engerman's enormously controversial *Time on the Cross: The Economics of American Negro Slavery* (1974).[5] Reviewed and debated in newspapers, magazines, and even on television, Fogel and Engerman's book is probably one of the most widely publicized and discussed academic works of the twentieth century. For those who supported the move toward a greater emphasis on numbers, their writings became a symbol of what was possible using quantitative methods in historical research. (Fogel was awarded the Nobel Prize in Economics in 1993 for his work in economic history.) For the critics, Fogel and Engerman's output demonstrated the pitfalls and, ultimately, the limits of quantification.

The 1970s and 1980s, in retrospect, were the high point for quantification's influence in the historical profession. As we shall see in the following chapters, by the 1990s quantification had virtually disappeared from the work of most historians in the United States (but not in Latin America). Economists and economics departments monopolized the key journals and professional associations, and their work employed mathematical and statistical skills in econometrics that very, very few historians attempted to master. A series of panels and debates at meetings of historians of Latin America in the 1990s now appear as the last gasps of the cliometricians in their efforts to persuade most historians (and humanists) writing about Latin America of the importance and validity of their work.[6]

In the United States, the influence of quantification came largely from the influence of economics departments and economists on the historical profession. In Latin America, the emphasis on quantification came not from economists but, rather, from the influence of the Annales School. This style of quantification has had a stronger and longer-lasting influence and a very different trajectory than in the United States. The scholarly and institutional connections between France and Latin America have formed a key part of the longstanding French cultural influence on Latin American elites. By the mid-twentieth century, a steady stream of Latin American historians and social scientists trained at French universities, especially in Paris (at a time when there were very few doctoral programs in history in Latin American universities).

Along with the Annales School, the rise of structuralism exerted enormous influence across Latin America. (Structuralists argue that deep, underlying systems and structures hold the true explanation for understanding societies and cultures. French intellectuals played a key role in the rise and influence of structuralism in the mid-twentieth century, especially in linguistics and anthropology.) Many Latin Americans completed degrees in France, and French academics often spent time teaching in Latin American institutions. In the 1930s, the state government created the Universidade de São Paulo (USP), for example, widely recognized today as the finest research university in Latin America, and French professors played a key role in the early years of the institution. Fernand Braudel (1902–1985), one of the greatest and most recognized historians of the twentieth century and one of the giants of the Annales School, taught in and helped organize the USP history department. Claude Lévi-Strauss (1908–2009), one of the founders of structuralism, spent his first years as a young professor of anthropology at USP and engaged in the fieldwork in Amazonia that would make him famous.[7]

While quantitatively oriented U.S. historians moved increasingly toward economics, econometrics, and modeling, their counterparts in Latin America stressed time-series data and structures. Many of them followed the example of Pierre Chaunu (1923–2009) whose massive statistical time series on Seville and its role in Iberoamerican trade (in collaboration with his wife Huguette) appeared in the late 1950s. Enrique Florescano (b. 1937), one of the most influential figures in the historical community in Mexico, did his doctorate in Paris in the 1960s and published his dissertation on the evolution of corn prices in eighteenth-century Mexico. In Brazil, the work of Maria Bárbara Levy on business and economic history and Maria Luiza Marcilio on demographic history are examples of the shift in the 1960s and 1970s to so-called serial history using carefully constructed statistical time series. Marcilio did her doctorate in Paris with Braudel and Levy did hers under the guidance of Frédéric Mauro. (Mauro and Chaunu were both students of Braudel. Chaunu spent the last years of his career at the University of Paris [Sorbonne], and Mauro held the first chair in Latin American history at a French university, the University of Paris [Nanterre].) The widespread influence of quantitative methods and the influence of the Annales School can be seen in the widely distributed manual on historical methods written by Ciro F. S. Cardoso (a Brazilian trained in France and working in Costa Rica) and Héctor Pérez Brignoli (an Argentine trained in France and working in Costa Rica). Originally published in Central America and Mexico in the 1970s, the book was widely utilized throughout Latin America. Mauro had mentored Cardoso and Pérez Brignoli completed his doctorate at the Sorbonne. When they wrote the manual, both historians were firmly in the social science, quantitative, structuralist camp.[8]

Quantification and quantitatively oriented historians formed a part of the larger move toward social history beginning in the 1960s. Although a number of earlier historical works clearly employed the methods and approaches of social history, these approaches became the overwhelmingly dominant ones among historians of Latin America. This dominance began to wane in the late 1980s and the profession took a major cultural turn by the 1990s. In the United States and Great Britain, a stress on quantification, empirical evidence (data), and social science methods mark the era of social history. As we shall see in the next chapter, these recede with the rise of cultural history. In Latin America, the turn to quantification is marked and sustained, especially in economic and demographic history, but the Anglo-American emphasis on empiricism is weak. One important reason is the historic importance of Marxism among Latin American intellectuals and academics.

Marxisms and Dependency Theories

The influence of Karl Marx (1818–1883) on historians and historical writing has been long lasting and profound in Latin America and Europe, but much less so in the United States. This influence in Latin America intensified after 1959 as revolutionary movements, right-wing dictatorships, and U.S. counter-insurgency efforts made the region one of the most politically volatile in the world. The Cuban Revolution seemed to foreshadow the possible triumph of socialist revolutionaries elsewhere in the region. The proliferation of multiple versions of Marxism among both armed revolutionaries and politicians made efforts to apply Marxism to history much more than an academic exercise. Salvador Allende, a Marxist, narrowly won the presidential election in Chile in 1970 and (for a brief historical moment) seemed to show that democratic Marxists could come to power (at least in some countries) in Latin America via the ballot box without the need to resort to armed revolution. In a broad sense, Marx's emphasis on "historical materialism" influenced those who looked to economic structures and material conditions of life as the keys to understanding politics and to writing history.

José Carlos Mariátegui (1894–1930) in Peru in the 1920s, Caio Prado Júnior (1907–1990) in Brazil, and Julio César Jobet (1912–1980) in Chile, beginning in the 1940s, are some early examples of prominent intellectuals deeply influenced by Marx.[9] By the 1960s, many varieties of Marxism influenced a wide variety of prominent historians across the region. Those taking a more traditional, materialist position (focusing on what Marx had called the base or infrastructure) tended to emphasize economic history, class struggle, and imperialism (mainly of the United States). The influence of Stalinism and the version of Marxism–Leninism promoted by the U.S.S.R. had its own followers, who engaged in a long-running debate attempting to show that Latin America during the colonial period was a feudal society and had to pass through a capitalist phase before socialist revolution was possible. Newer strains of Marxism, primarily from France and England, placed more emphasis on culture, ideology, and politics (Marx's "superstructure").

The importance of structures, economics, and Marxism all contributed in the postwar decades to the emergence of what became known in the 1960s and 1970s as dependency theory (in reality, theories). As the world recovered from the global devastation of the Second World War, many saw the nations and colonies around the globe divided into three "worlds."[10] The first was the industrial, democratic nations of the Global North led by the United States. The second was the industrial, socialist bloc led by the U.S.S.R., and the third consisted mainly of the colonies and nations of Asia, Africa, and Latin America (what some now call the Global South). Theorists characterized these colonies and former colonies as largely agrarian, with low levels of industrialization and urbanization and high levels of poverty. The first and second worlds were "developed" and the third "underdeveloped." An enormous literature emerged in various social science disciplines in the postwar period to explain how this global hierarchy had come about, and how to produce "development." In the age of the Cold War, this also became a debate over how to produce capitalist or socialist development. The past, for these policymakers, served as the prologue to the present and the future.

W. W. Rostow's classic *The Stages of Economic Growth: A Non-Communist Manifesto* (1960) presented the most influential capitalist version of the path to development. Taking the British model of industrialization (mid-eighteenth to mid-nineteenth centuries) and projecting it onto the world, Rostow argued that, to become developed, all countries had to move through a series of stages: traditional society, preconditions for take-off, take-off, drive to maturity, and high mass consumption. The countries of the Third World, according to Rostow's logic, remained stuck in traditional society. Only massive U.S. capitalist influence through aid and trade could help drag them (kicking and screaming) into the modern world. As a key advisor to presidents John F. Kennedy and Lyndon Johnson, his ideas had an enormous impact on U.S. policy toward Latin America and the rest of the Third World. In many ways, Rostow represented the essential distillation of modernization theory, the belief that the way to development for the Third World was to become more like Northern Europe and the United States.

For many modernization theorists this meant subscribing to a set of values – the Protestant ethic, individualism, and the profit motive. The rest of the world had to remake itself in the image of the North Atlantic model or remain "backward." The fear of the proponents of capitalist modernization theory was that the Third World would become fertile ground for leftist revolutionaries should these regions fail to modernize and remain mired in poverty. Social injustice and poverty, so the logic went, produced upheaval and unrest. Capitalist modernization would generate economic growth, a rising middle class, and democracy. The influence of modernization theory spurred scholars to examine the "middle sectors," their historical weakness in the region, and their potential for promoting democracy and capitalism. John J. Johnson, one of several historians of Latin America who worked for the U.S. Department of State in the 1950s, epitomized this approach with his *Political Change in Latin America: The Emergence of the Middle Sectors* (1958).

Dependency theories offered a powerful response to modernization theory. The path to development according to *dependentistas* was not capitalist modernization as in the supposed British or U.S. models. At its core, dependency theories argued that the "development" of the First World *caused* the "underdevelopment" of the Third World. They were two sides of the same coin. Rather than remaining "traditional" and failing to "take off," the underdeveloped world had been forced into the relationship of economic dependency on the First World. In short, the "developed" nations became rich through the systematic exploitation of the "underdeveloped" world, beginning with Europe's expansion outward across the globe in the fifteenth century. The core capitalist region (Northwestern Europe) created a world economy (for some, a world system) with the Latin American, African, and Asian colonies exploited and on the periphery.

Spain and Portugal, following this logic, had been pulled into a dependent relationship with Northwestern Europe despite the wealth generated by their global empires. They formed the periphery of the core. European domination of Latin America, Africa, and Asia made them truly the periphery of the periphery. Spain and Portugal locked Latin America into a dependent relationship even while England gradually exerted economic power over Spain and Portugal. The core (Northwestern Europe) consumed the raw materials of the periphery (gold, silver, copper, tin, cotton, dyes, and the like), transforming them into manufactured goods. By the nineteenth century, the argument goes, the industrial nations exported their surplus capital and manufactured goods to the periphery, in the process binding the new nations of Latin America into an unequal and dependent relationship. During centuries of colonialism, Spain and Portugal had been dependent on Northwestern Europe and Latin America on the Iberian metropolis. With independence in the nineteenth century, the colonies threw off Spanish and Portuguese colonial rule and soon found themselves under a new economic dependence – on Britain, France, and the United States. The economically and politically powerful core, through its local allies in the periphery, maintained these unequal terms of trade (commodities for manufactured goods). By the end of the nineteenth century the commodity-exporting countries of Latin America clearly depended on world markets (dominated by Britain and the United States) to purchase products they extracted and exported to the core (sugar, coffee, bananas, tin, copper, beef, wheat).

Dependency theories arose out of the analysis of these structural terms of trade, first through the non-Marxist writings of figures such as the Argentine economist Raúl Prébisch (1901–1986), who directed the Economic Commission on Latin America (in Santiago, Chile), and in the works of a wide variety of historians, some committed Marxists, others deeply influenced by various forms of Marxism. In some ways, dependency sought to explain why earlier theories of imperialism (especially the work of Lenin) seemed to explain the imperialism of the late nineteenth century but not the continued economic domination of the North Atlantic economies in the late twentieth century. Lenin had argued that imperialism was the final stage of capitalism and would lead to revolution across the globe in the twentieth century. Dependency theories emphasized global economic and political structures, and Marxist versions stressed the exploitative nature of commercial and then industrial capitalism. Newer forms of capitalism and imperialism not anticipated by Lenin at the dawn of the century had defused revolution both in the center (North Atlantic) and in the periphery. The obvious political response to these more sophisticated and nuanced forms of capitalist dependency was socialist revolution.

Two landmark works stand out in the vast literature on dependency. German-born, U.S.-educated Andre Gunder

Frank (1929–2005) wrote his doctoral dissertation in economics (on Ukrainian agriculture) at the University of Chicago under (of all people) Milton Friedman, the guru of conservative economics in the United States (neo-liberal economics to the rest of the world). After teaching at U.S. institutions in the 1950s, Frank spent much of the 1960s teaching in Chile, where he wrote *Capitalism and Underdevelopment in Latin America* (1967). Frank used the cases of Chile and Brazil to argue that capitalism created underdevelopment in Latin America. Chile in the 1960s also gave birth to the second (and even more sophisticated and influential) classic of dependency literature, Fernando Henrique Cardoso and Enzo Faletto's *Dependency and Development in Latin America* (1969).[11] Although the authors are a sociologist and an economist, and the book's subtitle is "essay of sociological interpretation," this slender volume is a sweeping historical analysis of the mechanisms of dependency with an emphasis on the twentieth century. Both works had enormous influence throughout Latin America and across the world, and dependency theories became perhaps the most important contribution of Latin America to the social sciences in the second half of the century.

The influence of dependency theories in Latin America was profound in all the social sciences and the humanities into the 1990s. Its impact was much more muted in the United States and Europe, although it was significant. In the U.S., Stanley and Barbara Stein's *The Colonial Heritage of Latin America* (1970) succinctly and eloquently synthesized the rise and evolution of Latin America's dependency in a widely read text of under 200 pages. Dozens of books in the social sciences in the U.S. took up the dependency theme. Perhaps the most widely read was the sociologist Peter Evans's *Dependent Development: The Alliance of Multinational, State, and Local Capital in Brazil* (1979). Building on the work of Cardoso and Faletto, Evans argued that new phases of dependency took shape in Latin America in the twentieth century. Despite industrializing and moving away from commodity exports, in the latest phase of development Brazil (and by analogy Latin America) remained dependent on the North Atlantic economies.

At a moment when it seemed that every academic work

coming out of Latin America had underdevelopment or development (or both) in the title, the influence of dependency was less marked in the United States. One of the bestselling textbooks of the 1970s and 1980s, E. Bradford Burns's *Latin America: A Concise Interpretive History* (1972), adopted an explicit dependency theory approach, as did a significant number of scholars who contributed regularly to the leftist journal *Latin American Perspectives* (founded in 1974). Dependency theorists studying Latin America even influenced a small group of scholars working on the history of the United States – in particular, Appalachia and the South.[12] In the end, dependency analysis was long on theory but short on empirical evidence. Although dependency had a large impact on theoretical approaches to Latin American history from the 1960s to the 1980s, there was very little intersection with the flourishing quantitative work on social and economic history.

The emergence of quantitative methods and dependency theories reflects the ascent of economics as a professional field, as well as the impact of the Great Depression, two world wars, and the Cold War. Together, these profound historical shifts across the first half of the twentieth century brought global economics to the forefront for social scientists and historians. For many, the shattering events that began in 1914 and reached a crescendo with the Second World War marked a massive global transformation from the laissez-faire, free-trade ideology of the British empire in the century before the First World War to a new world order dominated by U.S. economic and military power coming out of the Second. The Great Depression and the wrenching impact of the war gave birth to a global political economy in both the East and the West, with powerful government intervention and spending (especially on the military). The triumph of Keynesian economics to "prime the pump" and stimulate national economies through government deficit spending marked the ascent of economists as the experts who advised governments. The three decades of economic expansion from the 1940s to the 1970s appeared to confirm the triumph of economics and economists, until the great oil shocks, inflation, unemployment, and debt crisis burst the optimistic bubble of "scientific" expertise. In retrospect, the 1960s were the high point of the quantitative and economic turns for historians. Although the importance of economics and political economy had peaked by the 1970s, they would experience a smaller resurgence at the beginning of the twenty-first century.

4
The Social Turn

One of the striking characteristics of Latin American history has been its openness to influences from and conversations with the social sciences and humanities. Anthropology, sociology, political science, economics, literary analysis, and cultural studies – to cite the most obvious – have intermingled with historical work and influenced historians of Latin America, especially since the 1960s. In many ways, this cross-fertilization among disciplines has been even more prominent in Latin America, where academic disciplinary silos developed later than in the North Atlantic. Some of the landmark works of Latin Americans, especially before 1960, come from brilliant intellectuals who very often ignored disciplinary boundaries. In addition to the influence of economists on the quantitative moment and economic turn of the 1960s and 1970s, sociologists and anthropologists deeply influenced historians of Latin America after 1960. The turn away from diplomacy, high politics, military history, and elites to the enslaved, peasants, Indians, women, and other non-elite groups reflects this social turn. Although social history should include all groups in any society, from elites to masses, the social history of the late twentieth century overwhelmingly took as its focus non-elites.[1]

Comparative Slavery, Abolition, and Race Relations

Some of the most important areas transformed by the wave of quantification and social history were slavery, abolition, and race relations. These areas also have one of the longest histories of comparative transnational work in the Americas. For decades, a hemispheric conversation has connected scholars in these fields in the United States, the Caribbean, and Brazil, the three largest slave societies in the Americas. This conversation intensified after the Second World War. Gilberto Freyre's classic study of Brazilian slavery (1933) was translated into English as *The Masters and the Slaves: A Study in the Development of Brazilian Civilization* in 1944, but his work had already had influence on U.S. scholars (especially anthropologists) for at least a decade. Frank Tannenbaum, a sociologist at Columbia University, published the slim (but enormously influential) volume *Slave and Citizen: The Negro in the Americas* in 1946, and he compared slave societies in the U.S., the Caribbean, and Brazil (drawing on Freyre's work).

While these two classic works came out of a social science tradition based on interpretive analysis, institutions, law, and religion, Carl Degler's *Neither Black Nor White: Slavery and Race Relations in Brazil and the United States* (1971) showed the influence of demography and, more fully, of the new social history. Degler (1921–2014) was also consciously influenced by the civil rights struggles taking shape around him as he wrote the book. He was one of those rare historians of the United States who learned to read Spanish and Portuguese to carry out comparative work. The book won nearly every scholarly award in the academic community, as well as a Pulitzer Prize. Eugene Genovese (1930–2012), one of the most prominent historians in the United States in the last decades of the century, began his career as a committed Marxist before turning increasingly conservative and right wing in his later years. Genovese also learned to read Latin American scholarship in the original languages, and he produced the monumental *Roll, Jordan, Roll: The World the Slaves Made* (1972). Although a study of slavery in the U.S.,

Genovese drew on a larger, truly American literature, and his Marxist analysis of slavery had substantial impact in Latin America. Genovese's work also clearly demonstrated the turn away from elites (plantation owners) to the enslaved, as well as their impact and agency.

Slavery took shape across all regions of the Americas, and scholars took up studies in all regions of Latin America and the Caribbean, but the vast majority of the literature produced focused on the three largest slave societies. As Brazilian universities began to expand (slowly) after 1960, a prominent group of scholars began to transform studies of slavery, abolition, and race relations in Brazil. Initially, a small group of U.S. historians of Brazil made important contributions to this historiography, but by the 1990s Brazilians (logically enough) produced the bulk of the publications. Emilia Viotti da Costa (1928–2017), a Marxist scholar at the Universidade de São Paulo, transformed the field with her *Da senzala à colônia* [From Slave Quarters to the Colony] (1966), employing social and economic analysis in contrast to the emphasis in earlier writings on politics and ideology. Her work marked a turn to the agency of the enslaved, especially in driving the process of abolition (1888). Forced into exile by the Brazilian military regime, Da Costa moved in 1973 to Yale University, where until 1998 she trained several generations of U.S. historians who have written many important works on Latin America (and the United States).

The career of Kátia de Queirós Mattoso (1931–2011) illustrates the increasing interactions of scholars on three continents as the globe kept shrinking with a transportation and digital revolution in the last decades of the twentieth century. Born in Greece and educated in Switzerland and at the University of Paris – Sorbonne, Mattoso moved to Brazil in the 1950s, married a Brazilian, and settled in the city of Salvador da Bahia, where she became a professor of history. Profoundly influenced by the Annales School, her extensive work on the history of Bahia inevitably turned her to the history of Brazilian slavery. She published pioneering work on the social and demographic history of slavery, as well as the economic history of Bahia. In 1988, she was awarded the first chair in Brazilian history at the Sorbonne. Her *Etre esclave au Brésil: XVIe–XIXe* [To Be a Slave in Brazil:

Sixteenth to Nineteenth Century] (1979) sums up a vast new literature on slavery in Brazil with a clear social history approach. Her work moved Brazilian historiography from an older, essayistic tradition to more rigorous quantitative approach based on archival sources.[2]

Studies on slavery, abolition, and race relations rose dramatically in the 1970s and 1980s. Leslie Bethell's study of the abolition of the slave trade to Brazil (1970), Robert Conrad and Robert Toplin's on abolition (1972), and Stuart Schwartz's sweeping study of sugar plantation society in colonial Bahia (1985) are but a few indicators of the flourishing work in English. Much of this drew heavily on quantitative sources, especially local records from plantations, notaries, and courts. Trained under Schwartz in the United States, the Brazilian historian João José Reis published a pioneering study of a slave rebellion in nineteenth-century Bahia led by Muslims (1987), the first of many important works he would produce. A. J. R. Russell-Wood, a British scholar who taught for decades at the Johns Hopkins University, also began a long series of publications drawing heavily on local records in the state of Minas Gerais (1982).[3] Other scholars produced key works on important communities of African descent outside the three large slave societies.[4]

Studies of slavery and abolition also accelerated for the Caribbean, a region that the Spanish conquered in the sixteenth century, only to face the encroachment of the English, French, and Dutch in the seventeenth and eighteenth centuries. These imperial rivalries divided the Caribbean basin politically, linguistically, and culturally, while the islands shared the social and economic patterns of plantation agriculture. After the wars for independence in the 1810s and 1820s, Spain managed to hold on to Cuba, Puerto Rico, and the eastern two-thirds of the island of Hispaniola. It lost control of the remaining islands and enclaves on the Central and South American mainland (British Honduras and the Guianas – French, British, and Dutch). The imperial powers developed plantation agriculture and slave labor on nearly all the islands. The fragmentation of the Caribbean region contrasts with the political unity of the other two major slave societies – the Thirteen Colonies/United States and Brazil.

To be a comprehensive scholar of the Caribbean region, a historian has to master multiple languages and literatures.

The political and linguistic diversity also has given rise to a fascinating mix of historical methodologies as scholars from Britain, France, the United States, and the different islands have trained, collaborated and debated with and influenced one another. As in the case of other regions, some of the first important histories were written during the eras of imperial and colonial rule by (mostly elite) participants. Unlike most of Latin America, most of the island nations did not gain their independence until the twentieth century. The massive slave revolt in Saint-Domingue led to the creation of an independent Haiti in 1804, the world's first Black republic. The Haitians invaded, conquered, and then controlled the eastern side of the island until the 1840s, and the Dominican Republic did not finally consolidate its independence until the 1860s. Cuba and Puerto Rico remained under Spanish rule until 1898 and then came under U.S. control; in the case of Cuba, this lasted until 1902, while Puerto Rico is still an unincorporated territory of the United States. Most of the British, French, and Dutch possessions did not achieve independence until the late twentieth century.

The entry of these non-Iberian imperial powers in the seventeenth century and the different political trajectories in the succeeding centuries highlight the dilemmas of defining Latin America. Are the British, French, and Dutch possessions part of Latin America? Just until the arrival of the imperial rivals? Do they then leave Latin America once the Spanish lose control of the territory? Why include Haiti in Latin America, but not Guadeloupe or Martinique (or even Quebec)? Even if these areas are no longer part of Latin America, they provide us with multiple comparisons both among the colonies of the Spanish, British, French, and Dutch in the Caribbean and among the imperial possessions. In many ways, the Caribbean offers an array of possibilities for comparing slavery, abolition, and race relations over several centuries under differing political, linguistic, legal, and cultural regimes.

As in Brazil and the U.S., the scholarship produced after 1960 demonstrates the rise of social history and quantification.

The quantitative turn can be seen across the region as studies of slavery increasingly focused on demographic data – births, deaths, life expectancy, mortality, age structures. Scholars increasingly turned to local (as opposed to metropolitan) archives – plantations, notaries, parish registers – seeking to quantify with increasing precision in making statements about the slave trade and the material conditions of slave communities. Franklin Knight's *Slave Society in Cuba during the Nineteenth Century* (1970) and Kenneth Kiple's *Blacks in Colonial Cuba, 1774–1889* (1976) are examples of the move toward quantification. Herbert Klein's *The Middle Passage: Comparative Studies in the Atlantic Slave Trade* (1978) is part of a larger project (over several decades) to quantify the massive transatlantic slave trade over more than three centuries. The works of Rebecca J. Scott, *Slave Emancipation in Cuba* (1985), and Francisco Scarano, *Sugar and Slavery in Puerto Rico* (1984), are key examples of the scholarship on slavery and abolition by the 1980s. Many of these scholars were inspired by the pioneering work of the Cuban historian Manuel Moreno Fraginals on the sugar plantation system in the eighteenth and nineteenth centuries.[5] Turning to local records, demography, economics, and (when possible) specific enslaved persons, this social history began to provide us with a fine-grained and (sometimes) ground-level look at life in slave communities.

The increasing emphasis on agency generated many studies of resistance and rebellion in slave communities, such as Richard Price's *Maroon Societies* (1973). By the 1960s, there was already a long tradition of work on the most successful slave rebellion in the Americas, the Haitian Revolution in the 1790s. The classic book by the Trinidadian historian C. L. R. James, *Black Jacobins: Toussaint L'Ouverture and the San Domingo Revolution* (1938), anticipated this work by decades. After the French began to establish a foothold on the western side of Hispaniola in the seventeenth century, a long and complicated relationship with the Spanish side of the island took shape that continues to the present. This pioneering work on a French colony written by an English-speaking scholar from the British Caribbean shows the multilingual, multicultural, and transnational complexity of the Caribbean and its relationship to the field of Latin

American history. *Capitalism and Slavery* (1944), by a fellow Trinidadian, Eric Williams, is an equally momentous work whose influence transcends narrow definitions of geographic or regional definition. Williams (later the first prime minister of Trinidad) drew a direct linkage between the slave plantation economy of the Caribbean and the rise of British capitalism. His writings inspired countless other works on slavery and economic history, especially in the Caribbean. Both books remain in print today many decades after their initial publication.

Indigenous Peoples

The social turn to non-elites also spurred the development of a vast and expanding literature on the indigenous peoples of the Americas. Contributing to the field known as ethnohistory, in the United States two monumental studies bracket this period of immense growth and sophistication: Charles Gibson's *The Aztecs under Spanish Rule* (1964) and James Lockhart's *The Nahuas after the Conquest* (1992).[6] As seen in chapter 2, Gibson's contribution began with his 1950 Yale dissertation. Despite his visionary work, Gibson's principal sources remained those of the conquerors (in Spanish) and not those of the conquered (in Spanish and indigenous languages). The turn to locally produced indigenous sources would revolutionize the work of ethnohistorians.

Perhaps more than anyone else in the field, James Lockhart (1933–2014) transformed the study of colonial Spanish America, beginning in the 1970s. Trained in comparative literature as an undergraduate, Lockhart began by studying the conquistadors and ended up writing about the conquered. He made two fundamental contributions that helped shift the nature of the field – he actively pursued the use of locally generated notarial records produced by the Spanish, and, eventually, he turned to the local sources of the Indians of central Mexico in Nahuatl. Lockhart's *Spanish Peru* (1968) uses notarial records to reconstruct "social types," and in 1972 he published *The Men of Cajamarca*, a collective biography of the conquerors of Peru. Thereafter, his attention turned to Mexico and Indians. He taught himself Nahuatl (the language of the Aztecs, or, more precisely, the Nahua), trained several generations of historians to use Nahuatl sources, and produced a detailed, empirical style of history inspired by his social types terminology. In many ways, the work of Lockhart and his students bridges the old and the new. Still following the biographical, empiricist traditions of earlier generations, nonetheless, they are rarely interested in Spanish elites, institutions, or the imperial system. It is traditional in its heavy reliance on language and its historical evolution, but revisionist in turning to the languages of Native Americans (the "new philology"). Their approach is localized, fragmented, and at times self-consciously anti-theoretical.

The work on indigenous history reflects a long conversation between anthropologists and historians working on Latin America. Notably, in Mesoamerica and the Andes anthropologists developed a tradition of community studies and fostered an interest in the historical origins of contemporary cultural and social practices they observed in their fieldwork. After 1920, Mexican and U.S. anthropologists working in Mesoamerica began to build a long tradition of fieldwork among numerous indigenous groups. U.S. anthropologists such as Robert Redfield (1897–1958), Sol Tax (1907–1995), George Foster (1913–2006), and June Nash (1927–2019) spent long periods in the field, wrote prolifically, and trained generations of graduate students. In Mexico, Gonzalo Aguirre Beltrán (1908–1996), Wigberto Jiménez Moreno (1909–1985), Manuel Gamio (1883–1960), and Miguel León-Portilla (1926–2019) shifted the attention of scholars toward indigenous peoples, past and present. After 1960, historians increasingly turned to the study of indigenous peoples from pre-conquest times to the present. A powerful reflection of this shift is the emergence of the American Society for Ethnohistory, an organization that took shape after the Second World War and adopted the term ethnohistory in the mid-1960s.

The demographic analysis of the Berkeley School on colonial Mexico was a precursor of this work. Some historians, in effect, turned to pre-Columbian peoples and histories, especially the Aztecs and the Incas, and their work connected with that of archaeologists. In Mexico, the work of Pedro Carrasco Pizana (1921–2012) and Eduardo Matos Moctezuma (b. 1940) on pre-contact central Mexico reconstructed the history of the peoples of the Valley of Mexico before the arrival of the Spanish (pre-Latin American history?). In the decades after 1960, the history of native peoples in Mexico and the Andes blossomed, for the periods before and after the conquest. The works of the great Australian historian Inga Clendinnen (1934–2016) on both the Maya and the Aztecs are prime examples for Mesoamerica. Nancy Farriss's *Maya Society under Colonial Rule* (1985) reflects the pioneering work of Gibson and the influence of ethnography and archaeology. Subtitled "the collective enterprise of survival," the book demonstrates the complex and dynamic interactions between indigenous and Spanish societies and cultures in the three centuries after first contact, with the emphasis on indigenous agency and resistance.

The Andes attracted a truly international coterie of scholars working on pre- and post-conquest indigenous societies. John V. Murra (1916–2006), a Ukrainian immigrant to the U.S. who fought in the Spanish Civil War (1936–9), began to produce pathbreaking ethnohistorical work on the Incas in the 1950s. Murra documented the complex and intricate system of trade throughout the Andean world. Nathan Wachtel (b. 1935), who directed the École des hautes études en sciences sociales in Paris (founded by Braudel), produced the immensely influential *Vision of the Vanquished: The Spanish Conquest of Peru through Indian Eyes (1530–1570)*. In Peru, Franklin Pease (1939–1999) and Luis Valcárcel (1891–1987), among others, established a strong tradition of ethnohistorical work. In the United States, Steve Stern and Florencia Mallon (students of Emilia Viotti da Costa) began their careers in the early 1980s with major works on Peru. Their writings emphasized the agency of Indians and peasants. Stern analyzed the effects of the conquest on indigenous society. Karen Spalding's dissertation on Huarochirí, Peru, was one of the earliest and most influential in the move toward ethnohistory.[7]

Rural History

For most of its history, Latin America was an overwhelmingly rural society. At the beginning of the twentieth century, in nearly all the region, 85 to 90 percent of the population continued to live and work in rural areas. The land generated most economic and social activity, whether for local and regional consumption or for export to overseas markets. Consequently, the study of rural institutions and peoples has long been a major focus of the historiography. With the conquest of the core regions – the Caribbean, Mesoamerica, and the Andes – the Spanish crown established the *encomienda* system to handle the distribution of conquered lands. The *encomienda* was a grant for the *use* of land and the labor on it to an *encomendero*, who agreed to Christianize the local peoples, pay taxes, and protect the territory. In succeeding decades, the influx of new immigrants from Spain pushed outward from the core regions to new conquests in search of new lands to control. By the second half of the sixteenth century, the dramatic decline of the indigenous population forced the crown to move toward a new system – dividing up indigenous labor among the Spanish landowners – known as the *repartimiento* (*repartir* – to divide up). In Brazil, the crown granted enormous landholdings (*sesmarias*) to the early Portuguese settlers. These sixteenth-century systems laid the foundations of the land tenure system that would dominate in most areas of Spanish and Portuguese America until well into the twentieth century – a few powerful people (usually men of European descent) controlling large estates and the (non-European) laborers on that land. The great estates, known as *estancias*, *haciendas*, *fazendas*, plantations, *fincas* – and by many other terms – have been a major focus of historical research for centuries.

Before the social turn in the 1960s, the dominant approaches to the study of the great estates were primarily institutional and legal. The tendency was to study them from the top down, from an administrative perspective. The classic contribution (1952) by the French historian François Chevalier (a student of Braudel) on the formation of the great estates in Mexico was an early work (again the influence of the Annales School) that reconstructed the formation of the estates across centuries based an enormous amount of primary documents. He saw these great estates take shape out of the conquest, the rise of patriarchal *hacendados*, and he argued that the collapse of the native population and silver mining had turned the estates inward to become more self-sufficient and oriented toward local and regional markets. As Eric Van Young has pointed out, "Chevalier's great study flowered most exuberantly during a relatively brief period, between about 1965 and 1985."[8] Between the 1950s and 1980s, scholars furiously debated whether these estates and the export-oriented plantations (e.g. sugar, coffee) were feudal or capitalist ventures. This debate took on great political significance by the 1960s. For leftists and antiimperialists, this debate raised a fundamental question: how could one foment a socialist revolution if Latin America had not yet experienced full capitalism?

Much of this debate revolved around the forms of labor regimes on the estates. In Mesoamerica and the Andes, the bulk of the labor force consisted of indigenous peoples coerced into labor through legal mechanisms such as the *repartimiento* and its successor in the Andes, the *mita*. At the massive silver mines at Potosí in Upper Peru (now Bolivia), the exceptionally exploitative rotary draft labor system (*mita*) spanned large parts of the Andes. On the exportoriented plantations of the Caribbean and Brazil, enslaved Africans formed the bulk of the labor force. The social turn generated many studies of the estates, labor, and local society, providing a much more granular view of land and labor. Just as the revolution in studies of slavery produced a more nuanced picture of life in slave societies, these studies of rural society greatly expanded our understanding of life on the estates, their economies, and workers.[9]

The influence of anthropology, once again, played a key role after 1960. In addition to the growing number of studies of communities, especially in Mesoamerica and the Andes, historians and anthropologists turned their attention to the historical evolution of peasant society. Literally, peasants are "people of the land" – *campesinos/camponeses*. The flourishing school of peasant and community studies in the U.S.

dates back at least to the work of the legendary University of Chicago anthropologist Robert Redfield in Mexico in the 1920s and 1930s. By the 1960s and 1970s, the enormously influential anthropologist Eric Wolf (1923–1999) helped foster a vibrant debate about the very definition of the peasantry and the dynamics of peasant societies. Wolf focused on culture and power. His *Peasant Wars of the Twentieth Century* (1969) had enormous impact on debates about rural labor and the possibilities for social change in Latin America and the Third World. His best-known book, *Europe and the People without History* (1982), is emblematic of the turn away from the conquerors and elites to study non-elites such as Indians, slaves, and peasants. The Mexican anthropologist Rodolfo Stavenhagen (1932–2016) was another brilliant figure in the post-1960 decades generating hugely influential work on agrarian peoples and societies in Latin America. Stavenhagen's Jewish family (like Wolf's) had fled Nazi persecution in the 1930s. Educated at the University of Chicago, the Universidad Nacional Autónoma de México (UNAM), and the University of Paris, he was a truly cosmopolitan scholar.[10]

Perhaps the most famous of all the works on peasants was *Zapata and the Mexican Revolution* (1968) by John Womack, Jr. Placing *campesinos* and land at the center of the revolutionary upheaval, Womack depicted a charismatic and martyred figure and the "country people who did not want to move and therefore got into a revolution." Huge debates took shape around the very nature of rural labor and peasant societies. What were the defining features of these people? To what extent were they self-contained or participants in larger economies and social systems in Latin America? Were they by nature a conservative or a revolutionary force? Stuart Schwartz's *Slaves, Peasants, and Rebels* aptly synthesizes the historiographical trends and shifts in focus by 1990 – in particular, the turn to the lives of rural workers and their families and their agency and resistance to the powerful. Informed by many years working in Central America, Mexico, and Brazil, Ciro Cardoso in the 1970s and 1980s took up many of these issues with a deeply theoretical bent informed by his graduate training in France.[11]

Miners, Merchants, and Urban Workers

The silver and gold mines in Latin America formed a special type of great estate. Rather than producing the fruits of the land on farms and ranches, often on a vast scale, unfree Indians and enslaved Africans excavated gold and silver ore from the bowels of the earth under extraordinarily dire conditions. Although the European conquerors managed to find precious metals across much of the Americas, in the colonial period it was the silver mines of northern Mexico and Upper Peru (Bolivia) and the gold mines of southeastern Brazil that generated vast wealth for the elites while serving as economic engines for the Spanish and Portuguese empires. The gold and silver mines were also unlike many of the rural estates in that they became (at times) the sites of important urban centers. Potosí (to take the extreme case) in Upper Peru was possibly the largest city in the Americas in the seventeenth century, one that arose spontaneously around the mountain of silver known as the Cerro Rico (Rich Hill). Mining, especially silver mining, created the greatest fortunes in the Americas before the nineteenth century.[12]

Given its centrality to the Spanish empire, silver mining has been a focus of historical writings since the colonial period. Before the social turn, the tendency was to study it from an administrative or economic perspective. Hamilton's work on silver flowing into Europe is the classic example using metropolitan documents in Spain. Robert C. West, a geographer trained at Berkeley in the 1930s, undertook pioneering work on silver mining towns in northern Mexico and gold mining in Colombia before the boom. Scholars in Latin America, the United States, and Europe after 1960 produced increasingly sophisticated studies of mining in Spanish America relying on metropolitan, national, and local archives. David Brading's *Miners and Merchants in Bourbon Mexico, 1763–1810* (1971) – built on archival research in Seville, Madrid, Mexico City, and Guanajuato – re-created the complex world of the northern Mexican silver mines, labor, merchants, and the transatlantic economy. Peter Bakewell's *Miners of the Red Mountain* (1984) is one of the finest studies of Potosí, with an emphasis on the Indian labor force. The Argentine historian Enrique Tandeter (trained in Paris by Ruggiero Romano) drew on the abundant work of the previous three decades to produce *Coercion and Markets* (1993), a highly sophisticated analysis of the role of Potosí stretching across much of Spanish South America.[13]

While silver mining largely employed heavily capitalized industrial operations and underground works in New Spain and Peru from the mid-sixteenth century on, gold and diamond mining flourished in eighteenth-century Brazil and then largely faded by the nineteenth century. With very few exceptions, gold and diamond mining involved hydraulic works on the surface and rarely underground mines like those in the silver centers in Spanish America. Panning, diversion of streams, and shallow tunneling characterized most gold mining operations. The more ephemeral nature of gold mining sites left fewer institutional records at the local and imperial levels. As a consequence, studies of gold and diamond mining in Brazil focus on the eighteenth century, and primarily on enslaved labor and the economic impact of mining on Brazil, Portugal, and the Atlantic world. The great English historian Charles Boxer set the "gold standard" for these works with the publication of *The Golden Age of Brazil, 1695–1750* (1963). Despite his unorthodox career and very traditional training, Boxer's sweeping work anticipates the social and economic history boom that followed. As the largest concentration of enslaved labor in the Americas in the eighteenth and nineteenth centuries, Minas Gerais has generated a steady and increasingly rich historiography, but primarily among those interested in slavery, not in mining. The gold mining zone has generated a long list of rich examples of the influences of comparative slave studies, demographic history, social history, and the Annales School influence in Brazilian academia. One outstanding example is Laura de Mello e Souza's brilliant work on the impoverished masses who toiled in the midst of the great wealth around them.[14]

Along with powerful landowners, merchants were among the wealthiest and most powerful figures in Latin America, and the wealthiest merchants were those engaged in long-distance commerce, especially across the Atlantic. This pattern is generally true well into the twentieth century, even as the region became less rural and more urban. As countries industrialized (most notably, Brazil, Mexico, and Argentina), the role of the great estates and large landowners remained important, but the majority of the population (especially after 1940) moved from the countryside into the burgeoning cities. The massive peasantry shrank as the ranks of the urban working class and poor mushroomed. In the second half of the twentieth century, the elites diversified from being landowners and merchants to becoming bankers, financiers, corporate executives, and industrialists. The middle classes grew and social structures became more diverse and complex, as we shall see in the next chapter.

The merchants who attracted the greatest attention in the colonial era have been those engaged in long-distance commerce. In Spanish America, these merchants were often vital to the closed colonial trading system that for centuries flowed exclusively through Seville, with key ports at Havana, Veracruz, Cartagena, Panama, Lima (Callao), and Santiago de Chile. In the Portuguese empire, the system was also closed to outsiders but was more global (and porous), stretching from Salvador da Bahia and Rio de Janeiro to Africa, the Indian Ocean, and East Asia. Merchants engaged in the commerce of the enslaved, sugar, dyes, silver, gold, and diamonds, most notably. Like most professions in this early modern world, the merchants had their own guilds to protect their interests, and some of the earliest scholarship in the twentieth century focuses on these institutions. In the post-1960 decades, scholars delved deeply into the collective biographies of those engaged in commerce, especially those in the principal ports and population centers.[15]

With independence in most of the region in the early nineteenth century, the old mercantilist system collapsed, opening Latin America to international commerce with all nations, although, in practice, this largely meant Great Britain and the United States. The influx of foreign capital, technology, expertise, and business altered the social landscape of the region, but the changes would come slowly and fitfully. After a brief foreign investment bubble in the 1820s burst, most of the region faced decades of internal conflict and reordering. An enormous literature over the last half century has debated the political impact of independence (was it really a watershed or simply "same horse, new rider"?); the insertion of Latin America into the world economic system (which did not happen in most countries until after 1870); and who benefited from the creation of the new nation-states (not the indigenous and rural masses). Much of the social history up until the 1990s focused not on the heroes of independence (a key concern of pre-1960s scholarship) but on the impact of independence and nation-building on non-elites.[16]

Under the influence of dependency theories, many scholars stressed the power of the "external connection" and foreign business interests, especially after 1870. They traced the rise of new elites and the impact of these shifts on Indians, slaves, and the racially mixed masses. On a macro-level, foreign capital received enormous attention, especially levels of investment, trade, technology, and profits. Curiously, despite the importance placed on the negative impact of foreign capital on Latin America, very few scholars chose to study foreign enterprises or entrepreneurs. The sub-field of the history of business (foreign and domestic) remained very small at the end of the twentieth century. The anti-elitist, anti-foreigner bent of the scholarship generated many studies of non-elites, but very few of those often deemed responsible for the underdevelopment of the region and the reinforcement of the massive social inequalities.[17]

Rather than study firms and managers, numerous scholars turned in droves to the history of workers, especially urban labor. Looking back, the period from 1970 to 2000 was a sort of golden age of Latin American labor history. Overwhelmingly, the early studies focused on labor unions, understandably, where the archival materials were richest and best organized. As we have seen, historians have long studied rural workers – on haciendas, on plantations, and in mining operations. The emergence of incipient industrialization in the nineteenth century and its surge in the twentieth – especially after the 1930s – gave rise to a significant urban working class, especially in Mexico, Argentina, and Brazil. In these three large countries, and in many others, the major shift took place after 1929 as more and more governments (especially under the influence of populism) created labor ministries and legalized the creation of unions. Many of the early studies tended to see these "populist" regimes (Lázaro Cárdenas in Mexico, Juan Perón in Argentina, Getúlio Vargas in Brazil) as coopting and controlling labor movements after the 1930s.[18] Populist leaders often are depicted as demagogues who manipulated the burgeoning urban masses.[19] By the 1990s, revisionists reacted with studies showing the agency of these workers, their roles in creating the labor structures, and their resistance to government control. While early works emphasized the unions and their struggles, by the 1990s studies turned increasingly to working-class culture and consciousness.[20]

Latin American labor history lagged in its development behind work on Europe and the United States. Hobart Spalding's enormously influential synthesis, *Organized Labor in Latin America* (1977), and Charles Bergquist's *Labor in Latin America* (1986) stood as early landmark publications that sought a comparative history across nations. As James Brennan has pointed out, the so-called new Latin American labor history since around 1990 "has celebrated the diversity of the national experiences and found the explanations for the distinct trajectories of the labor movements in history and culture."[21] The first half-century after independence and recent decades have received much less attention than the period from the late nineteenth century to the 1960s. Studies of the early twentieth century often emphasize the ideological battles between anarchists and socialists in the early union movements. The largest and richest literature has been about the years from the era of populism from the 1930s to the 1960s and the so-called new unionism after 1970.[22] As we shall see in the next chapter, with the cultural turn in the 1990s, scholars looked increasingly to the study of worker consciousness, discourse, and culture and away from the material conditions of life that had dominated in the age of social history.

Women and Gender

Labor history, like social history in the last decades of the century, also turned increasingly toward the history of women, gender, and sexuality.[23] In the United States, a generation of scholars (primarily women) produced a wave of works on women in Latin America. Asunción Lavrin (b. 1935), a Cuban-American historian, stands out as one of the foremost pioneers in this field. Her personal and professional trajectory in the 1960s and 1970s is emblematic of women in the field. She was among the first cohort of women completing a doctorate at Harvard (1963) and then engaged in part-time teaching, research, and writing as she moved with her husband from Berkeley to Chicago to Washington, DC, while rearing two children. In the 1970s, she eventually took on a tenured position first at Howard University and subsequently at Arizona State University (1995–2007). Her early work on religious women in Mexico was some of the first in an ongoing genre that continues half a century later. In the 1970s, she began to produce work on the social history of women in colonial Mexico, eventually broadening to other areas of Spanish America. Over five decades, Lavrin published a series of important monographs and important edited volumes. The growing number of women in the field after 1970, no doubt, spurred a growing interest in women's and gender history. As with the wider field of women's history, much of the early work on Latin America sought to make women visible as historical actors.[24]

The waves of women's movements and feminism after 1960 stimulated the emergence and development of the history of women, family, gender, and sexuality. Much of the early work focused on the colonial period, especially women whose lives were reasonably well documented, such as nuns and elite women (e.g. Doña Marina/La Malinche, the mistress of Hernán Cortés, and Sor Juana Inés de la Cruz, the brilliant writer and nun in seventeenth-century Mexico). As was the pattern in much of Latin American history, scholars turned first to well-established archives from religious orders, the Inquisition, and legal records. In broad strokes, much of the early work emphasized male domination of women, the limitations of women's options, and exploitation. That work over the past few decades has been increasingly nuanced, drawing on many more sources (especially notarial and court records) to reconstruct the lives of non-elites and with a strong emphasis on agency and resistance.[25]

By the 1980s, work on family, marriage, class, ethnicity, and non-elite women became increasingly important. Historians produced a good deal of work on indigenous and enslaved women. The publications by Silvia Arrom and Patricia Seed on Mexico, Donna Guy on Argentina, and Verena Martínez-Alier (Stolcke) on Cuba and Brazil are examples of the growing sophistication of women's and gender history by the 1980s.[26] These early works often retained influences from the demographic and quantitative trends of the 1960s and 1970s and are clearly within the wave of social history. Scholars in Latin America generated a vast and rich literature on all aspects of women's history looking at the struggle for rights, women's roles in political movements, and female roles, from wives and mothers to prostitutes and factory workers.

Although scholarly collaboration across the Americas continued to increase with improved travel and communications, differences clearly marked the interests and orientations of scholars in the United States and Latin America. While U.S. power and interventions in Latin America and the first two waves of feminism profoundly influenced women's history in the U.S. academy, in Latin America the often damaging impact of U.S. power in conjunction with several decades of authoritarianism gave the historiography in the two regions different trajectories. Much of the work in Latin America turned to women's roles in political movements, revolutionary struggles, opposition to dictatorship, and the struggle for human rights. Although feminism affected the direction of the literature in Latin America, much of women's and gender history would be more deeply influenced by French theorists (Foucault, Derrida, Kristeva). The influence of Marx remained strong, although in new forms.[27]

One very important form of work that began to emerge and that brought together scholars from many disciplines was oral histories and "testimonial" literature. Although these were studied by many scholars in different disciplines and fields, an important subset were the stories of women, especially non-elite females. Perhaps the most controversial *testimonio* was *I, Rigoberta Menchu: An Indian Woman in Guatemala* (1984), recorded and edited in collaboration with the Venezuelan anthropologist Elisabeth Burgos-Debray. Margaret Randall's interviews with women in Sandinista Nicaragua and Moema Viezzer's interviews with a political activist married to a Bolivian miner are excellent examples of this very influential genre. Daniel James's *Doña Maria's Story* (2000) is an excellent example of oral history accompanied by a highly sophisticated discussion of the genre, its importance and limitations.[28]

As the next chapter will discuss, the 1980s and 1990s, nevertheless, mark a transition that reflected larger trends in the profession – a move from women's history to the history of gender and sexuality. As in other areas of Latin American history, the cross-fertilization with the social sciences brought together scholars across disciplines to produce a rich literature in women's and gender studies.

Institutions: New Perspectives

With the rise and dominance of social history, some traditional areas of research receded in importance, and some took on a whole new look. The institutions that had played such a large role in the field in earlier decades continued to receive attention, but from new angles influenced by the trends of quantification, social history, and (eventually) the cultural turn. These shifting trends are clearly evident in work on the Catholic Church and religion.[29] One of the most powerful and pervasive institutions in the Iberian world and in the creation and evolution of Latin America, the Catholic Church received a great deal of attention from the very beginnings of the field. Traditional studies focused on the institutions of the Church, its operations, and its theology. From the 1960s to the 1990s one can see the historiographical shifts, sometimes even within individual careers. Nancy Farriss (b. 1938) began her career with a monograph on relations between the crown and clergy in colonial Mexico (1968) before turning to pioneering work in Mesoamerican ethnohistory, including a fine-grained study of the give and take between clergy and indigenous peoples in the processes of evangelization.[30]

The "spiritual conquest" of Latin America has also been a major theme since the beginnings of the field. Robert Ricard's classic study (1933) of the spiritual conquest of Mexico was a brilliant early work (once again from the Annales School) that envisioned the process of evangelization largely from the perspective of the clergy as they, in his view, carried out "a rapid and near-complete Christianization of the natives."[31] With the emergence of ethnohistory after 1960, the cultural clash and processes of religious interactions among native peoples, Afro-Latin Americans, and Iberians attracted many outstanding scholars. Overwhelmingly, these studies demonstrated the incomplete nature of Christianization and the spiritual conquest. Central to much of this scholarship over the past half-century has been debate over the very nature of these processes and the results. To what extent did evangelization eradicate indigenous and African beliefs (survivals), produce mixed results (syncretism, creolization, blending, transculturation), or give rise to new religions and belief systems? From an even broader perspective, did Latin America experience a long-term secularization of society, as was long posited for Europe and the United States? In short, did religion and religious beliefs become less important over the last five centuries? These debates have engaged historians, anthropologists, and those in religious studies for decades.

Much of the work up to the 1990s reflected the influences of structuralism and an emphasis on the continuity in beliefs from pre-conquest times up to the nineteenth and even the twentieth century. To cite but a few examples, Serge Gruzinski (b. 1949) over the last forty years has taken up where Ricard left off and produced a series of important works on the complex processes of evangelization and Christianization in Mexico (continuing the long French tradition in Latin American history). His work has stressed the mixing of beliefs, a sort of cultural *mestizaje*. The brilliant work of Inga Clendinnen on the Maya of the Yucatan reveals the complexities of cultural clash and limits of our ability to recover the worldview and culture of the vanquished. Many of the students of James Lockhart have mined colonial sources in indigenous languages to provide us with a much fuller picture of conquest and cultural clash than earlier scholars who worked only in European languages.[32]

Although traditional political and military history fell from grace during these decades, scholars continued to produce excellent studies of politics and the military. Civil wars in Central America in the 1980s and authoritarian regimes across the region spurred new work. The Argentine political scientist Guillermo O'Donnell's pathbreaking *Modernization and Bureaucratic-Authoritarianism* (1973) is one of the most important works of dozens that reflected an intense cross-disciplinary conversation about the nature and history of authoritarianism in Latin America. The upheavals in Central America, for a brief period, drew many young historians to undertake research on the region, joining a small but dedicated group that had long worked on its history. James Dunkerley's *Power in the Isthmus: A Political History of Central America* (1988) is a fine example of some of the contributions to the history of Central America after 1980.

Studies of institutions did not disappear after the social turn, but historians now examined them through new lenses: economics, collective biography (prosopography), how law functioned in daily life rather than as text. A series of scholars delved deeply into the economic basis of Church institutions, providing us with detailed studies, especially of the economic activity and wealth of religious orders.[33] Studies of religious orders and clergy became more sophisticated and moved from the institutional and biographical to examine social types, gender, and processes of evangelization. William Taylor's masterful *Magistrates of the Sacred* (1996) epitomizes this type of work at its most sophisticated.

In the 1970s and 1980s, historians produced a series of studies of colonial administration under the influence of social history. In one of the most notable examples, two scholars, Mark Burkholder and D. S. Chandler, quantified the very old discussion about the replacement of creoles with *peninsulares* under the Bourbon Reforms in the eighteenth century. This long-term and systematic discrimination against creoles had long been cited as a key cause for the wars for independence in the early nineteenth century. In one graph summarizing their data set (nearly 700 *audiencia* ministers from 1687 to 1808), they provided precise numbers that showed the extent and duration of this shift.[34] Legal history had long been one of the most traditional fields of study in Latin American history, especially in Latin America. In the late twentieth century, historians turned from studies of the laws and legal theory to how the law functioned, in practice, on the ground.³⁵ The cultural turn would build on these studies and take them in new directions after 1990.

Institutionalization of the Field

The proliferation of textbooks, journals, and reference tools by the 1990s provides us with clear signs of the consolidation and maturation of the field of Latin American history in the United States. With the expansion of college enrollments and offerings in most major universities of courses on Latin America, the demand for textbooks grew. Richard Graham's survey entitled *Independence in Latin America* (1972, rev. edn, 1994), Bradford Burns's *Concise Interpretive History of Latin America* (1972, and nine more editions as of 2016), and Benjamin Keen and Mark Wasserman's *Short History of Latin America* (1980, and many other editions), are but a few examples. By the 1980s, scholars in the U.S. were producing synthetic histories of the colonial period, the nineteenth century, and the twentieth century, a sign of specialization and the growing volume of scholarship. *The Cambridge History of Latin America* (a massive eleven-volume project that would not be complete until 2009) got under way in the 1970s under the wise editorship of the British historian Leslie Bethell (b. 1937) shortly after the publication of the landmark *Latin America: A Guide to the Historical Literature* (1971). The *Colonial Latin American Historical Review* (1992) joined the venerable *Hispanic American Historical Review* (1918), providing an important additional venue for publishing historians.

The British had also constructed a vibrant and excellent community of historians of Latin America by the 1990s, although it was much smaller. In addition to Oxford and Cambridge, at least half a dozen other universities employed historians of Latin America and most also had centers for Latin American studies. The Society for Latin American Studies (1964) has its own *Bulletin*, and the excellent *Journal of Latin American Studies* (1969) serves as the key journal for historians as well as for other fields of Latin American studies. On the continent, France continued its long tradition (dating back to the early twentieth century), with several chairs in Latin American history in French universities. A few other European universities also had regular positions by the 1990s. In Latin America, where there had never been a shortage of scholars and scholarship, by the 1990s universities in most countries had fully developed doctoral programs producing a steady stream of professional historians who found jobs in the expanding universities. By the end of the century, Latin Americans produced the overwhelming majority of scholarship in the field.

The 1970s and 1980s also mark the acceleration of interaction among scholars on all three continents, as Latin Americans trained in graduate programs in the United States and Europe (mainly England and France), and as U.S. and European scholars spent more time in Latin America as researchers and teachers. One effect of the tight job market in the North was the permanent migration of some U.S. and European scholars to positions and careers in Latin American universities. By the beginning of the twenty-first century, the emerging digital revolution and the global expansion of air travel would fundamentally alter the interactions among historians across continents. Reflecting larger world patterns, even as the academic world became more globalized, national academic communities became more defined.

5
Cultural and Other Turns

Fin de Siècle

Just as the Cuban Revolution, the revolutionary upheavals of the 1960s and 1970s, and the oil shocks shaped the global context in which historians wrote about Latin America, world events also influenced historical production after 1980. In Latin America, escalating interest rates in the early 1980s followed the oil shocks of the 1970s, sending the region into a massive debt crisis. Governments across Latin America found themselves unable to meet loan payments, international banks shut off new credit, and nearly all the region experienced a "lost decade" of economic contraction rivaled only by their experience during the Great Depression of the 1930s. The rise of Ronald Reagan in the United States and Margaret Thatcher in the United Kingdom ushered in a new era in economic policymaking dominated by neo-liberalism, a new form of classic economic liberalism (what is called conservative economics in the United States). After a half-century of government interventionism, "inward-oriented growth" through import substitution industrialization, and trade protectionism, nearly all Latin America (and much of the world) moved toward downsizing government, reducing public spending, removing trade barriers, and creating more open markets. Globalization and neo-liberalism became the watchwords of the new era. In Latin America, Chile under General Augusto Pinochet's authoritarian regime dove off the deep end and created one of the world's most open economies by dramatically reducing trade and financial barriers while privatizing most state-controlled enterprises and many agencies (such as social security). At the other end of the spectrum, Cuba remained the most closed and statist economy in Latin America. Most countries lay somewhere between these two extreme ends of the spectrum.

Ironically, the most sweeping wave of democratization in the history of Latin America accompanied the wrenching transformations of the debt crisis and the neo-liberal turn. By October 1973, nearly all the nations of Latin America had fallen under some form of military or authoritarian rule except for Costa Rica, Colombia, and Venezuela (and Mexico's "one-party democracy"). In the 1980s and 1990s, nearly all these repressive regimes gave way to some form of electoral politics, however flawed. With the electoral defeat of the Sandinistas in Nicaragua in 1990 and the collapse of the Soviet Union soon thereafter, the cycle of leftist revolutionary upheavals that had begun in the 1950s came to a close. In what now seems a moment of naïve euphoria and optimism, many commentators declared the end of socialism, the triumph of capitalism, and a new world order, with just one superpower – the United States. Democracy, capitalism, and peace, for these commentators, had emerged triumphant from five decades of cold war. Latin America seemed to fall off the radar screen of most of the United States public with the end of the civil wars in Central America, a pattern reinforced in the aftermath of September 11, 2001, as the United States turned its attention to the Middle East.

The end of right-wing military regimes, flawed democratization, neo-liberal economics, and the sudden disappearance of revolutionary socialism formed the backdrop of historical writing on Latin America from the 1980s through the first decade of the twenty-first century. These global events stimulated rethinking about the old area studies approach that had emerged in the 1960s. For some leftist scholars, area studies had emerged out of the Cold War, along with U.S. government efforts to guide and direct research, and they called for its rejection. Many social scientists criticized area studies as an outdated obstacle to knowledge creation in a globalized world. They argued for an abandonment of the study of regions in favor of research around big themes that could be applied around the globe. This methodological shift profoundly affected research opportunities, as funding shifted from a focus on world regions to thematic research across regions. For historians with their traditional grounding in deep knowledge about place, the focus on themes across global regions reduced funding opportunities.[1]

In the United Kingdom, Thatcher's neo-liberalism wreaked havoc in universities as they faced budget cuts and downsizing. For Latin American studies, this meant a reduction in the number of research centers, the consolidation of others, and a declining number of positions. A generational shift took place as those scholars trained in the 1960s and 1970s retired and many were not replaced. In the United States, the field of Latin American history remained small (within the larger profession) but steady until the Great Recession of 2008–9 drastically reduced university positions for younger scholars. In Latin America, in general, the 1990s and early 2000s were years of gradual expansion – of universities, graduate programs, and doctorates granted – until the Great Recession.

A Cultural Turn?

Just as social history dominated the period from the 1960s to the 1980s, cultural history emerged in the 1980s to become the most important approach in the field by the 1990s. As with social history, the category of cultural history is broad, vague, and more indicative of an emphasis on culture than a definable methodology. The so-called cultural turn in the late twentieth century has been much debated and generated a cottage industry of publications on how to define it, when it began, and if it has ended.[2] Although historians of Latin America employ many different approaches and methodologies, cultural history has dominated for the last three decades, especially in the United States. The shift is clear in Latin American history, away from some of the most important focal points of the era of social history – quantitative and empirical data, structures, and larger narratives – to an emphasis on experience, identity, discourse, and microhistories. At the same time, other historical approaches have flourished, some that begin to challenge the very definitions and categories of Latin American history. Scholars of borderlands and Atlantic world history, notably, have produced a rich historiography that crosses older field boundaries and definitions. Works on empire, networks, and transnational flows have challenged both traditional categories, such as the nation-state, and the boundaries that once existed between Latin American and Latinx studies.

In the words of the eminent Annales historian Roger Chartier, in the 1980s the profession moved "from the social history of culture to the cultural history of society."[3] Although many scholars have written about a linguistic and cultural turn in academia, the terminology, chronology, and meaning of the shifts in the late twentieth century have been hotly debated. The broader influences on the historical profession are clear: literary and cultural studies, linguistics, anthropology, and the "posts" – post-modernism, post-structuralism, and post-colonial studies. None of the last three (like the cultural turn) can be neatly defined, and the extent of their influence across fields and countries varies widely.

From a broad historiographical vista, the move from the social to the cultural is a shift from an emphasis on the material, empirical, structural, and class as a social category to language, discourse, ritual, and class as experienced and constructed through meaning. In some ways, the methodological shift is from the sociological to the anthropological – that is, from social organization to cultural experience. Culture, in this sense, is about making meaning, and for many historians the cultural approach aims to decode language, text, and discourse to analyze the processes of making meaning for human individuals. As the British historian Peter Burke has succinctly put it, the "common ground of cultural historians might be described as a concern with the symbolic and its interpretation."[4]

The more materialist approach before the 1980s tended to privilege the structures and processes of society and economics over language, discourse, and symbols. In its most crass formulations (such as uncreative forms of Marxism), the objective base (infrastructure) generated the subjective world of words and symbols (superstructure). Culture, in this sense, was epiphenomenal. The cultural turn stands this scheme on its head. Culture is not reflective of the material, nor is it epiphenomenal, but constitutive of reality. Central to this approach is the search for how historical actors see, define, and respond to the world around them. Like social history, the "new" cultural history continues to study marginalized peoples and their agency but focuses on discourse, narrative, and representation versus the material realities of social history. In broad strokes, it opposed the cultural to the social, the micro- to the macro-level, and subjectivity to structure.

Most of the key influences in the cultural turn are European theorists, primarily French – Michel Foucault (1926–1984), Jacques Derrida (1930–2004), and Pierre Bourdieu (1930–2002) – and the Italian Antonio Gramsci (1891–1937). Gramsci, a committed Marxist and one of the founders of the Communist Party in Italy, spent many years in prison under Mussolini's fascist regime. Decades ahead of the cultural turn, Gramsci filled his prison notebooks with brilliant theoretical analysis of Marxism with an emphasis on culture and ideas. In particular, he formulated the concept of hegemony, one that would become very influential in the late twentieth century, long after his premature death. Moving beyond the simplistic materialism of many Marxists, Gramsci argued that the key to the power of many ruling elites was their ability to forge a cultural, moral, and ideological leadership over those less powerful and subordinated groups (often called subalterns). The power of the state, for example, was not simply force or physical coercion but also cultural hegemony.[5]

Pierre Bourdieu has exerted widespread influence across many disciplines in the humanities and social sciences, especially history, sociology, anthropology, and communication studies. Bourdieu sought to bridge the worlds of structure and agency and to discern how both contributed to social identity. He aimed to bring together both the empirical and the theoretical in a "theory of practice." One's *habitus*, following Bourdieu, consists of habits and dispositions, and it is the way a person understands the world and reacts to it. A person accumulates these habits and dispositions from the surrounding environment and then uses them to make choices. For Bourdieu, our everyday "practices" can demonstrate improvisation or agency, with "the framework of schemata inculcated by the culture in mind and body alike."[6] Individuals construct themselves through the acquisition of what he called cultural, social, and symbolic capital. People forge their own path, but within larger structural constraints. To paraphrase Karl Marx, from another century, people make their own history, not under circumstances of their own choosing but under circumstances "given and transmitted from the past."[7]

Foucault and Derrida emerged as influential intellectual figures in the French academy in the 1960s. By the 1980s, they exerted enormous sway over scholars in many fields across multiple continents. Their work is enormously rich, complex, and (many would argue) abstruse. Foucault's oeuvre has the greatest impact in work on "regimes of power," and Derrida's influence is in his method of textual and linguistic deconstruction. Derrida systematically attacked the dominant structuralism of the postwar decades. While structuralists sought to uncover the deep-seated underlying patterns in human societies (such as kinship structures for Claude Lévi-Strauss), their critics dismissed this as illusory. They attacked the structuralists for constructing a world of "false" universals and binaries (e.g. sacred/secular, modern/traditional). For the post-structuralists, language and signs are flawed and imprecise, and all meaning is inherently unstable. Following the literary theorist Roland Barthes (1915–1980), not even the author can be sure of his or her own textual meaning. In a world where all language is unstable, all narrators are unreliable, and all authority is decentered, the very possibility of writing history becomes suspect.

Foucault's examination of the history of madness, medicine, incarceration, and sexuality has exerted enormous influence in many fields. At the heart of much of his work is the relationship between power and knowledge – how those with power create and shape knowledge to establish regimes of control, whether in politics, sexuality, or medicine. Like Derrida (with whom he had a long feud) and Barthes, Foucault contributed to what has been loosely labeled post-modernism.

Like post-structuralism, it is more of an approach or method of critique than a philosophy. Post-modernism began as a critique of what had been considered foundational for modernism and the modern period – Enlightenment rationality, grand narratives, universals, and a belief in an objective reality, truth, and progress. At its core, post-modernism is a form of zealous skepticism that attempts to deconstruct all categories and systems of knowledge emphasizing relativism, the instability of meaning, and the impossibility of establishing any objective reality.

Like the other "posts," post-colonialism is a broad and often confusing group of approaches that emerged in the last decades of the twentieth century. Its influence is more pronounced in cultural and literary studies than in the historical profession. It has a long genealogy, often traced back to the writings of intellectuals such as Frantz Fanon (1925–1961), Aimé Césaire (1913–2008), and Albert Memmi (1920–2020), all of whom were born and raised in French colonies (Martinique and Tunisia). Edward Said (1935–2003) and Gayatri Spivak (b. 1942) are two of the most influential exponents, the first a Palestinian-American literary critic and the second an Indian philosopher who has been a professor at Columbia University since 1991. Said's *Orientalism* (1978) and Spivak's essay "Can the Subaltern Speak?" (1988) are two of the iconic works seeking to deconstruct the very notions of colonialism, the colonizer, and the colonized.[8] Said's enormously influential work critiqued Western writers since the eighteenth century who created the very concept of the "Orient," their biases and worldviews, bringing into question the geographical and cultural areas that have formed the dominant conceptions of East and West. For Said, Orientalists constructed the West as rational, developed, and superior, in contrast to the undeveloped, static, and inferior East.

Writing from her perspective as an Indian woman, Spivak, and a brilliant group of colleagues, relentlessly demolished traditional perspectives of the British empire and the very notions of empire, colony, and nation. In her essay on the subaltern, she explores the possibility of finding the voice of those subordinated and oppressed by imperial officials, when the documentary base that has survived (at best) offers a mediated voice and (at worst) silences the subaltern's voice. For historians, the question is a profound one: how can we recover the voices of the masses of people throughout the history of Latin America when the power structures of colonialism have erased, stifled, and garbled their voices?

For the critics of the cultural turn, this path leads to a disconnect between the hard empirical realities of life and an academic community lost in its own theorizing that privileges the fragments of history over the whole. The harshest critics of post-modernism and the cultural and linguistic turn argue that the adherents have lost their way in a maze of linguistic confusion, muddled reasoning, and navel gazing. With the rise of neo-liberal capitalism, the collapse of the Soviet Union, and the retreat of socialism, for some of the critics, the longstanding political struggle seemed to evaporate into fragmented disputes over identity politics, cultural representation in the new regimes, and the loss of direction in decades-long battles for social justice and economic equity.

Latin American History and the Cultural Turn

The influences of the turn to culture generated both fierce debates among historians of Latin America in the United States in the 1990s and serious reflection on some of the methodological approaches of the previous few decades. The *Hispanic American Historical Review*, the oldest and most prestigious of journals in the field in the United States, published a group of articles in 1999 that effectively summarizes the major issues.[9] Although focused on the rise of a "new cultural history" in the writing of the history of Mexico in the United States, the exchanges between proponents and opponents sum up the shifting nature of the field at the close of the twentieth century. Eric Van Young's essay brilliantly captures both the promise and the perils of the "colonization" of the field by cultural history as many in the profession attempted to move beyond structures, dependency theory, materialism, and meta-narratives of previous decades. At its core, anthropology deeply influenced the new approach (an anthropological turn?) and the move to study culture not as a coherent and comprehensive system of norms but as conflicted and contested. Cultural history then becomes the reconstruction, especially among the subaltern, of the formation of meaning for individuals and their relationship to power. It concentrates on language, identity, beliefs, and symbolic systems. As Van Young points out, "Whereas we once arrayed ourselves as observer and object, we now have two subjectivities warily circling each other, or even three if the maker of the source-text is distinct from the actors being described."[10]

Rather than see nations, states, gender, sexuality, or other foundational concepts as fixed or certain, historians turned to the ways in which they had been imagined, constructed, or invented in specific historical times and places. In his essay in the journal, William E. French boldly states that those "participating in the crafting of the new cultural history of nineteenth-century Mexico are interested, above all, in 'imagining' or, perhaps more accurately, in 'imaginings.'" Perhaps the most striking imagining was of the new nations of the Americas in the nineteenth century. Even as many historians criticized grand narratives, others focused on the ways non-elite groups, as well as elites, sought to construct nations. The work of Eric Hobsbawm and others made the case for envisioning the nation as a modern (post-1750) phenomenon that is a cultural construct. The publication of Benedict Anderson's brilliant and concise *Imagined Communities: Reflections on the Origins and Spread of Nationalism* (1983) spawned many, many followers. For Anderson, the nation emerges out of a group of people, most of whom will never meet face to face, imagining that they share common traits and a common history. Although he placed Latin America at the forefront of his discussion of nationalism, highlighting the role of "Creole Pioneer" elites in the wars for independence, historians of Latin America rejected his analysis of the region while often embracing his notion of imagined communities.[11]

As the critics of the cultural approach in the *Hispanic American Historical Review* argue, these methods can lead to the abandonment of objectivity, confused concepts, and an intrusive and narcissistic historian/ethnographer. They also see this approach as another way to inject personal (leftist) politics into historical methodology. A widely cited essay by Florencia Mallon in the *American Historical Review* epitomizes the position of the leftist historian of Latin America in the 1990s with the end of leftist revolutions, the "slow death" of the Cuban Revolution, the sudden demise of the brutal Shining Path movement in Peru, and the enormous wave of neo-liberalism. As Mallon puts it, "what is a progressive scholar to do?" She then goes on to a sophisticated analysis of the pros and cons of subaltern studies and its applicability to Latin America. Speaking from her own experience, she acknowledges that those attracted to Marxism in the 1960s and 1970s may have fallen into a "methodological trap." "Dismissing earlier works and traditions as irrelevant and passé," she concedes, "we often missed important clues concerning the explanatory power of ethnicity, race, family, ecology, and demography because our newly discovered theoretical correctness told us that it all came down to class and mode of production."[12] Mallon's 1994 essay epitomizes the shift (especially among scholars in mid-career in the 1990s) from the social to the cultural. She, like Van Young, emphasizes the need to balance the archive and fieldwork with literary and textual analysis.

These essays in the late 1990s also reflect the emergence of a "new political history" deeply influenced by the turn to culture. The social turn had consciously repudiated the "old political history," often criticized for its focus on the politics of elites and nation-states. Although political history did not disappear after 1970, its importance receded in the age of history from below, structuralism, and materialism. The "new" political history continued the commitment to non-elites (subalterns) and, under the influence of the cultural turn, sought to reconstruct their politics, especially their relationship with the emerging nation-states of the nineteenth century. Historians sought to recover the role of marginal peoples in the creation of hegemonic practices and to reexamine the relationship between the state, culture, and Gramscian hegemony. As Van Young noted in his *HAHR* essay, this presents serious challenges for the historian seeking to recover the ideas and beliefs of those masses of people who often appear in documents only as a result of their encounters with the state apparatus – courts, churches, the Inquisition, notaries. These are the challenges at the heart of Spivak's influential essay "Can the Subaltern Speak?." Ironically, the move from seeing subalterns as victims to emphasizing their agency runs the risk of turning them into the rational, self-interested actors that historians have so often criticized in the methodologies of the social sciences.

Some of the most interesting, influential, and creative work in this new political history has been on the relationship between common people, nation, state, and politics. Florencia Mallon's *Peasant and Nation* (1995) takes the bold step of comparing a series of locales in both Peru and Mexico, while Peter Guardino's *Peasants, Politics, and the Formation of Mexico's National State* (1996) focuses on the state of Guerrero. These, and many other works, turn to the granular, local level to reconstruct the language, politics, and agency of peasants. What did liberalism, nationalism, or the nation mean to people in their daily lives and struggles? Gilbert Joseph and Daniel Nugent's edited volume on modern Mexico, *Everyday Forms of State Formation* (1994), and Joseph's edited volume *Reclaiming the Political in Latin American History* (2001) became key reference points for historians taking the cultural turn and those writing a new political history.

As the U.S. historians writing in the *HAHR* issue note, they had taken a cultural turn that historians in Latin America had largely not taken. By the end of the twentieth century, even as communications more directly connected historians across the Atlantic world, the growth and sophistication of scholarship increasingly reinforced diverging trends across countries. Even as the new political history took a cultural turn in the United States, new forms of political history took shape in Latin America that redefined politics, concentrating on sociability, public opinion, and the public sphere. These trends fundamentally transformed our understanding of the nineteenth century, especially the transition from colonies to nation-states. The history of the era of the wars for independence that had once been the domain of heroes and great men now became a vibrant transformation of political culture for all levels of society. Elections, once dismissed as meaningless and corrupt, now took on a new life as vibrant arenas of political activity, and scholars turned to forms of sociability and associations as important arenas of politics. Where once the dominant narrative had been one of exclusion, elite domination, and manipulated elections, scholars began to see widespread participation (despite hierarchy and inequality) in the language, debates, and struggles over liberalism, constitutions, and sovereignty.

Many of these Latin American scholars were deeply influenced by Jürgen Habermas's notion of the public sphere. Beginning in the 1960s, Habermas (b. 1929) argued that the eighteenth-century Enlightenment fostered the creation of a public sphere, outside the control of the state, where individuals could exchange and debate rational knowledge and opinions free of coercion. The emergence of salons, associations, print culture, clubs, and the like provided multiplying venues for the proliferation of a bourgeois culture of discourse.[13] Although contentious discussions took shape over the very definition of the public sphere, whether there was one or many in a nation in the nineteenth century, and the relationship of the public sphere to the "market" and the "state," Habermas's theorizing stimulated a large and rich literature.

In *The Many and the Few* (2001), for example, Hilda Sabato astutely analyzed nineteenth-century elections and participation in public life as means of rethinking political participation and the rise of democratic politics in Argentina. The common thread through many of these studies is the effort to recover the voices of the masses, often through newspapers and magazines, theater, and judicial records. Rather than seeing Latin America as filled with nations that failed to modernize politically, these scholars show there was a real shift across social strata in the normative framework from seeing the people as subjects of the king in the colonial period to citizens claiming popular sovereignty in the new republics. An older tradition focused on citizenship as seen through progressive enfranchisement. More recent studies continue to study voting and elections (especially the ground-level mechanics of the processes) but with a much richer and multilayered understanding of citizenship. Public opinion, sociability, and the public sphere offer additional ways to recover the political voices of the masses as well as those of elites. Sabato brilliantly and concisely synthesizes the work in *Republics of the New World: The Revolutionary Political Experiment in Nineteenth-Century Latin America* (2018). Sabato and other scholars have argued that the region became one of the most radical and innovative centers of liberal and republican politics.[14]

While Sabato is influenced by the work of Habermas, she sees limits to the applicability of the public sphere to Latin America. Pablo Piccato, a Mexican historian who teaches at Columbia University, has perhaps been the leading proponent of work on the public sphere in Latin American history.[15] In contrast to the cultural turn among historians in the U.S., and their focus on culture and identity, Piccato argues for a revaluing of meaning and social structure. For Piccato, the "public sphere was a universally accessible conceptual place where private citizens came together to discuss matters of common interest, on the assumption that reason, the only requisite, was evenly distributed, and that their voices would have an impact on public opinion." In participating in this public sphere, citizens would bridge "the private realms of domesticity and work, the publicity required to exchange opinions with others in civil society, and the state."[16] The public sphere, following this line of theorizing, is a space outside the privacy of the home but also beyond the functions of the state apparatus. While he recognizes that many were excluded from this exchange, mainly on the basis of gender and class, Piccato argues that the public sphere places the emphasis more on politics than on culture and thus provides a means of bringing together the voluminous research on specific places and the pursuit of larger syntheses on nationalism and representation.

Perhaps the most influential scholar in this area has been François-Xavier Guerra (1942–2002), born in Spain, trained by François Chevalier at the Sorbonne, and later professor there. Turning away from the structuralism of the 1960s and 1970s, Guerra focused on what he saw as the transition from tradition to modernity, and he applied the concept of the public sphere to nineteenth-century Latin America. His *México: del Antiguo Régimen a la Revolución* (1988) and *Modernidad e independencias: ensayos sobre las revoluciones hispánicas* (1993) placed the public sphere at the center of the transformations of the nineteenth century in Latin

America. His work explicitly puts culture at the center of the analysis in contrast to the structural, social, material, and class analysis of the previous generation of historians. These works also reflect a trend toward the revival of intellectual history after several decades of disfavor. In a sense, scholars of the public sphere lean more toward the history, meaning, and circulation of ideas than the history of culture and its relationship to power.[17] While the new cultural historians tend to emphasize fragmentation and divisions, scholars of the public sphere see the rise of public opinion, imagined communities, and nations. Both groups have brought the nineteenth century, especially the wars for independence and the transition from colonies to nations, back from several decades of scholarly neglect.

These historians of ideas and politics have also revitalized the idea of citizenship, making it a rich and innovative focus of scholarship. Similar to work in the social sciences, this literature has broadened the idea of citizenship far beyond the traditional notion of voting rights and even civil rights. Much like the British theorist T. H. Marshall (1893–1981), scholars envision citizenship as including civil, political, social, and even cultural rights. The wave of democratization in Latin America since the 1980s, and its limits, have drawn scholars in history and the social sciences to rethink the meaning of citizenship not only in recent times but in the nineteenth century as well. The emphasis on agency, culture, and the lower classes has generated a vibrant scholarship, especially on the relationship between the lower classes and the formation of nineteenth-century nation-states.[18]

Popular culture has been one key area of vibrant research. The turn to popular culture began in the 1960s even before the so-called cultural turn of the 1980s. As with so many key concepts, there is no consensus on its meaning. Does "popular" refer to the masses, the lower classes, those rituals and symbols that are widely shared? What is the relationship between popular culture and elite culture? Despite the definitional quandaries, historians of Latin America have produced a rich literature on film, visual arts, folklore, food, religion, music, media, dance, and many other topics that have examined the meaning of popular culture, how it takes shape, who shapes it, and its relationship to learned or elite culture. Jeffrey Pilcher's work on the history of food, Eric Zolov's on music and counterculture, and William Beezley, Cheryl Martin and William French's edited volume *Rituals of Rule, Rituals of Resistance: Public Celebrations and Popular Culture in Mexico* (1994) are but a few examples of the creative and innovative ways historians have written about popular culture in recent decades.

The study of popular culture has also produced some of the most fruitful conversations across disciplines since the 1980s. The work of the anthropologists Clifford Geertz (1926–2006) and Néstor García Canclini (b. 1939) has exerted enormous influence on historians. Geertz famously called for "thick description," something clearly more accessible to the ethnographer of the contemporary world than the historian chasing after scarce documentation of subalterns in the archives. García Canclini, an Argentine long resident in Mexico, has written astutely about popular culture and its relationship to globalization, nation-making, and the media.[19]

Gender and Sexuality

The turn to culture in Latin American history (as in the larger profession) also shaped the development of studies of gender and sexuality. In the age of social history, women's history emerged as a field with an emphasis on recovering ("making visible") the often ignored roles and deeds of women and women's organizations (such as religious orders). Social historians sought to recover the lives of non-elite women, especially through demographic and institutional records (parish registers, wills, court cases, religious orders). The turn to culture and identity and the notable influence of Foucault turned scholars' attention away from the history of women to studies of gender and sexuality. As with the new cultural history, the turn to gender has been more pronounced in the United States than among scholars in Latin America.[20] Joan Scott (b. 1941), the eminent U.S. historian of France, played a key role in the emergence of gender as a category of analysis and deeply influenced many historians of Latin America who turned to gender history. Following Foucault, Scott argued that gender was socially and culturally constructed, "the understanding produced by cultures and societies of human relationships." Gender history, by definition, is not about women but about all genders, and at the core of all history.[21]

The political upheavals of the 1960s and 1970s, the differing impact of waves of feminism across the Americas and Europe, and the specific historical conditions across so many countries affected the development of women's studies, women's history, and the history of gender and sexuality. One clear trend was the role social scientists played in the development of women's studies among Latin Americanists and the slower development of the historical scholarship.[22] The work of social historians in the 1960s and 1970s (noted in chapter 4), especially on demography, family, and class, reflected the quantitative, structural, and materialist trends of the times. By the 1990s, historians turned to culture, experience, meaning, symbols, and rituals under the influence of the cultural turn. Among historians of Latin America working in the United States, gender had become one of the most creative and dynamic areas of research by the 1990s.[23]

Scholars have analyzed how gender was experienced especially in daily life, its relationship to power, and in institutions such as the church and state. As with others who have made the turn to culture, the influence of Foucault, Gramsci, and Bourdieu is evident in a wide range of works. At times, these influences made historians (such as Steve Stern's *The Secret History of Gender*, 1995) increasingly theoretical in their scholarship and anthropologists (such as Ana María Alonso's *Thread of Blood*, 1995) more historical in their approach. What is common to virtually all work on gender and sexuality over the past few decades is the understanding that these categories are socially and culturally constructed. For many historians, the goal has been to deconstruct the categories for specific times and places, to uncover how individuals "have navigated the terrain of gender in their daily lives." In Foucauldian terms, they seek to recover the genealogy of institutional and discursive systems. In destabilizing, decentering, and historicizing gender across so many regions and periods, this work has enormously complicated the use of classic concepts over the span of Latin American history. Some, for example, have complicated our understanding of patriarchy, a concept so central to the history of Latin America and to gender relations.[24]

Some of the most innovative work has examined the relationships between gender, class, and race/ethnicity. *The Making of the English Working Class* (1963), by E. P. Thompson, has exerted enormous influence, not only on labor historians but also on cultural historians writing about class. Published before the cultural turn, Thompson's landmark book influenced historians across Europe and the Americas. (He also became a vocal critic of much of the theory behind the turn to culture in the 1980s and 1990s.) Although Thompson was a Marxist, his writings on class hinged on working-class culture, and he envisioned class not as structural but relational, built on experience. An emphasis on relationships and experience was central to many studies of gender, race, and sexuality by the 1990s. In broad terms, historians in the U.K. tended to focus more on class and those in the U.S. more on race, while in Latin America the emphasis was on both race and class with an emphasis on the latter.

Enormous debates took shape over which should be primary in historical and social science analyses, class or gender. The revolutionary upheavals, especially in Central America in the 1980s, stimulated reassessments of women, gender, and development especially by leftist scholars. Much of the early work of social scientists focused on women and issues of development. The influence of Foucault, particularly in Latin America, resulted in studies of discourse and knowledge regimes, especially how states and reformers sought to construct and regulate public spaces, morality, and identities. Studies of prostitution, criminality, and public health, for example, provided detailed and rich new contextualization, especially of lower-class women.[25]

The longstanding French influence on studies of mentalities and a new style of cultural history in the French academy, along with Foucault, can be seen in studies of sexuality among historians in Latin America.[26] For the colonial era, Inquisition records have played a crucial role in efforts to reconstruct sexuality and gender, especially for the lower classes. In Brazil and Mexico, Luiz Mott, Ronaldo Vainfas, Laura de Mello e Souza, and Solange Alberro were pioneers, in particular in using these records to reconstruct ideas about gender and sexuality. Church and legal records have been central to research over the past few decades on family, marriage, gender, and sexuality.[27] Many of the early studies in women's history relied heavily on these records, and demographers drew much of their data from parish registers. Since the mid-1980s, historians have mined these records to reconstruct gender roles, sexual mores and practices, and the experiences of common people. One of the most fertile areas of research has been honor, its meanings and role in Latin America over centuries.[28]

The focus on gender and sexuality also generated important pioneering studies of (especially male) homosexuality. Here, again, the influence of anthropology played a key role in a dialogue with history. As ethnographers produced studies of contemporary society and culture, historians worked to reconstruct same-sex relationships all the way back to the conquest and even the pre-conquest era.[29] Although most gender history continues to focus on females, studies of masculinity and non-binary genders have become more common.

Indigenous History

The impact of the turn to culture had a much less visible impact on studies of the native peoples of the Americas. As we saw in chapter 4, the influence is most striking in studies of the conquest (especially of Mesoamerica and the Andes) and of the cultural shifts among indigenous peoples, especially during the colonial period. The works of Inga Clendinnen and Serge Gruzinski on the "spiritual conquest" or of Nancy Farriss on the Maya of the Yucatan in the 1980s reflect the influence of anthropology and the turn to symbols, rituals, and meaning. In the United States, the influence of James Lockhart and his many students has played a large role in the work of those studying Mexico and Central America over the past forty years. Lockhart trained his students in Nahuatl, and what he called the New Philology, a careful reconstruction of language and its changes over time. The first wave of clergy learned local languages and created Roman alphabets, and then native peoples gradually used this new writing system to record their own lives. With this linguistic and paleographic expertise, historians have scoured the rich local ("mundane") documents, especially of Mexico, to produce detailed studies of many locales from the perspective of the indigenous peoples.

Some of the most innovative studies have fundamentally revised our understanding of the Spanish military conquests of the sixteenth century and of the centuries-long and ultimately incomplete spiritual conquest of native peoples. The work of Matthew Restall, Susan Schroeder, Camilla Townsend, and Ross Hassig, for example, has brought to the fore the roles of indigenous peoples (men and women) in the conquest – those allied with Spaniards and those fighting them.[30] Kevin Terraciano, Louise Burkhart, Victoria Bricker, and David Tavárez, to name but a few, have enriched our understanding of religious and cultural exchanges among many of the peoples of Mesoamerica (Nahua, Zapotec, Mixtec, Maya). Turning to indigenous-language documents, rereading old Spanish texts, and bringing to them a nuanced cultural sensitivity, a number of historians have helped us rethink the military conquest. We now have a greater understanding of indigenous perspectives on the conquest, their roles, and the long-term impact on indigenous communities from Mexico to the Andes.

The rise of identity politics and multiculturalism in Latin America over the last quarter-century has stimulated studies of the role of indigenous peoples in the formation of nation-states and their place in those states in recent decades. As Rebecca Earle has shown in *Return of the Native* (2007), in the nineteenth century, many new nations in Latin America romanticized the indigenous past, much as in the United States. Indianist novels formed a powerful strand of romantic literature until the rise of realism in the 1870s. Realist and naturalist novels sometimes focused on the oppression of Indians, especially in Mexico and the Andean republics. *Indigenista* movements emerged in the 1920s and 1930s, in Mexico with the triumph of the revolution, and in Peru with the rise of Raúl Haya de la Torre (1895–1979). These movements aimed to recognize the value and importance of the indigenous heritage of the nation, especially through art, museums, and literature. In recent decades, a new form of indigenism seeks to gain full political and cultural participation of indigenous peoples as citizens, particularly in those Latin American nations with historically significant native populations, such as Mexico, Guatemala, Colombia, Ecuador, Peru, and Bolivia.

While social scientists have produced studies of citizenship and politics focusing on recent decades, historians have looked back and revisited the relationship between indigenous peoples and the nation-state. Some of these works begin in the late eighteenth century with major challenges to the Spanish empire, most notably the massive rebellions of Tupac Amaru and Tupac Catari in the Andes. Works such as Eric Van Young's *The Other Rebellion* (2001) bring the techniques of social and cultural history to recast the role of Indians in the bloody struggles for Mexican independence. One of the richest fields of research has been a reexamination of the relationship between state formation and indigenous peoples in the nineteenth and twentieth centuries.

As with social history, cultural history at the turn of the century continued to place emphasis on recovering the history of non-elites – the poor, the enslaved, workers, indigenous peoples – and brought gender analysis to the center of historical analysis. In the quarter-century or so after 1980, historians on both sides of the Atlantic, North and South, engaged in vibrant debates and produced highly sophisticated work. As with social history, cultural history generated new approaches and innovation and dominated historical work, but it did not push out all other approaches. Political history flourished in new forms, cultural history influenced more sophisticated approaches to social history, and many other more traditional fields continued, and even thrived. Latin American history became methodologically and theoretically more diverse, and historians in the field also became more diverse, with increasing numbers of women, Latinx, and black graduate students and professors.

As the historical profession in Latin America grew dramatically, and as methodological influences varied in strength across many nations, the differences between works produced in the U.S., Europe, and Latin America became more pronounced – even as communication across national historical communities intensified. By the beginning of the twenty-first century, amid globalization and the apparent waning of nationalism, creative new historical fields had emerged that challenged the very boundaries of Latin American history and presaged the redefinition of the field.

6
Beyond Latin American History

A New Century, a New Millenium

As the twentieth century came to a close, the number of historians of Latin America probably numbered around one hundred in Europe, more than a thousand in the United States, and in the many thousands in Latin America. Doctoral programs in Latin American history had spread across all three continents, and university-trained historians produced the vast majority of the thousands of books published in the field each year. The enormous growth of higher education in Latin America by the early twenty-first century and, with it, the rapidly expanding number of university professors of history have led to a constantly increasing asymmetry in research and publications. Understandably, the publications produced by scholars not residing in Latin America is a smaller and smaller proportion every year in comparison with that produced by scholars in Latin America. At the same time, the transportation and communication barriers that once loomed so large across these continents have diminished dramatically – first, with a revolution in air travel and then with a digital revolution. The speed and intensity of contacts, collaboration, and exchanges in research, teaching, and publishing have shifted substantially since 1980.

The expansion of the professoriate has also generated

greater specialization. This has produced two, seemingly contrasting, developments: that historians are more likely to focus their research on one country, and that more and more historians, mainly those working on pre-independence centuries, have rejected the confines of the nation-state to work on transnational, imperial, or transatlantic topics. The staggering amount of primary materials in national, regional, and local archives that has become available, along with the flood of publications in monographs and articles, has made it less and less possible to master the materials and historiography of more than one nation in the post-colonial centuries. The publication demands for academic historians seeking tenure and promotion also push them toward greater specialization and publication in an expanding number of specialized academic journals. At the same time, more and more historians, especially in the anglophone world, have pursued work that challenges traditional borders and national boundaries. This is most notable in the fields of Atlantic world history, the history of borderlands, and studies of immigration. The crossing of traditional boundaries and regions has also made it more difficult to categorize many publications as Latin American history. These trends contribute to the ongoing debate about the very definition of the field.

Borders and Frontiers

One of the most vibrant areas of research in the United States since the 1980s is the field of borderlands history. As we saw in chapter 2, the field has a long history going back to the early twentieth century and the pioneering work of Herbert Eugene Bolton. Bolton trained his graduate students as historians of the Americas (not just the United States), with a focus on the regions in the eighteenth and nineteenth centuries where the Spanish, French, and British empires expanded into the North American interior and clashed – with each other and with native peoples. Despite his fascination with priests and conquistadors, Bolton took Native Americans seriously and wrote about their relationships with the conquering Europeans. By the 1960s and 1970s, the last of his students had reached retirement, and most of them had eventually situated themselves professionally within the community of historians either of the United States or of Latin America. Bolton's desire for a history (and historians) of the Americas writ large gradually gave way in the face of specialization and professionalization in the academy. In the 1980s and 1990s, a new generation of historians seized the borderlands legacy and completely transformed it.

The new borderlands history looks back to Bolton, but without the romanticism that imbued his tales of missionary priests, conquistadors, and Indians. For many of these historians, the frontier is a place where political and cultural borders are undefined or unclear, while borderlands are contested areas at the frontiers of empires and nations. Bolton's approach included indigenous history as key to the history of the region. Recent studies have reoriented the field and often place indigenous peoples at the core of the analysis and the narrative. The rise of a new indigenous history and new western history in the U.S. has had a large impact on borderlands research for those who see themselves primarily as historians of the U.S. or of Latin America.[1] As with social history, these works often focus on peoples once viewed as marginal. As with the new cultural history, many of these historians look to the ways people create meaning and how cultures are contested and constructed. Historians of the borderlands tend to emphasize social fluidity, cultural mixing, and syncretism. As in much of the profession, this history has turned away from grand narratives and toward micro-history, to the extent that we now have a vast historiography rich in local studies but short on works that seek to place these studies in a larger framework.[2] The field had attracted so much attention by the close of the twentieth century, and the notion of borderlands had been applied to so many other regions of the globe, that some scholars feared the concept had become overused and abused.

Although many scholars contributed to the growth of borderlands history in the late twentieth century, David J. Weber (1940–2010) was perhaps the most important figure. Trained as a historian of Latin America at the University of New Mexico, Weber focused in his work largely on what today is the U.S. Southwest, but when it was largely under

Spanish or Mexican rule. *The Mexican Frontier, 1821–1846: The American Southwest under Mexican Rule* (1982) and *The Spanish Frontier in North America* (1992) stand out for their use of both U.S. and Mexican archives, as well as the sensitive analysis of Indians, Mexicans, Tejanos, and Anglos in this region long claimed by Spain and Mexico and then incorporated into the United States. His *Bárbaros: Spaniards and Their Savages in the Age of Enlightenment* (2005) is a masterful analysis of the struggle of indigenous peoples to shape their own destiny as they resisted the encroachment of Europeans into their lands for more than two centuries after the conquest of central Mexico. Weber's work spanned Latin American, U.S., and western history, as well as indigenous history and Chicano studies. Like much of the work on the borderlands, it required work in multiple languages, countries, and archives and knowledge of many different communities of historians.

Some of the most impressive works have placed indigenous peoples at the center of the analysis rather than employing the traditional approach of the expansion of empires (France, Spain, Britain) or nation-states (Mexico, the U.S., Canada) into the region with the destruction of native peoples and cultures. Pekka Hämäläinen's *The Comanche Empire* (2008) and Brian DeLay's *War of a Thousand Deserts* (2008) both seek to tell the story from the interior looking outward, and not the outside looking inward. Richard White's now classic *The Middle Ground: Indians, Empires, and Republics in the Great Lakes Region, 1650–1815* (1991) inspired much of this work. Raúl Ramos's *Beyond the Alamo* (2008) and Andrés Reséndez's *Changing National Identities at the Frontier* (2004) beautifully examine the many different peoples, but especially Spanish-speakers in Texas and New Mexico as they shift from Spanish, to Mexican, to U.S. control. Ramon Gutierrez's controversial *When Jesus Came the Corn Mothers Went Away* (1991) is an early example of efforts to recover the history of the diverse peoples of the region through an analysis of marriage and sexuality in what today is New Mexico.

The emphasis in many of these studies on cultural fluidity, entanglements, shifting identities, and ethnic diversity for the era of empires and their collapse in the nineteenth century carries over into work on the twentieth century. The orientation of most of these scholars has been to the field of U.S. history, and only rarely to the community of historians of Latin America. The growth of Chicano and Latino studies, the new western history, indigenous history, immigration studies, and transnational history have all contributed to the expansion of borderlands history and, in turn, have been shaped by the new historiography over the past thirty years. Works like Samuel Truett's *Fugitive Landscapes* (2006), Rachel St. John's *Line in the Sand* (2011), and Oscar Martínez' *Border People* (1994) quite literally straddle what became the U.S.–Mexican border in the mid-nineteenth century.

Transnational History

As historians turned to the movement of peoples across all sorts of fluid borders and boundaries during the era of empires, scholars have also taken a transnational turn de-emphasizing the role of the nation-state and highlighting the movement of peoples across national borders. More and more studies trace the stories of people moving between nation-states, and their transnational sagas no longer fit easily into conventional categories of U.S. or Latin American history. Gabriela Soto Laveaga's *Jungle Laboratories: Mexican Peasants, National Projects, and the Making of the Pill* (2009) is an outstanding example of ways to span borders and more traditional definitions of fields of study. The shifting nature and porosity of political boundaries over the past two centuries highlight the problems both of labeling the work of many of these historians and of the very definition of Latin America and its history. Indeed, most of the historians cited in the last few paragraphs would probably not think of themselves as historians of Latin America. As millions of people have moved north out of the Caribbean, Central America, and Mexico into the United States, the effort to label historical work on them becomes more complicated and, ultimately, not very useful. The field of American studies has grappled with its own identity for several decades as many in the field have sought to make it less "United States studies" and to take in more of the Americas.[3]

Some of the most vocal advocates of transnational history have declared the demise of history built around nation-states and called for more work that emphasizes transnational themes as opposed to taking the nation and national narratives as the basis of historical research. The move toward transnational history has grown with the increasing awareness of globalization and its impact on communities, large and small, around the world.[4] Although the movement of peoples around the globe has gone on since the human species began, it clearly accelerated after 1492, and the Americas played a key role in this early, foundational phase of globalization. Long before national borders emerged in nineteenth-century Latin America, people, animals, and microbes flowed across vast areas that are now nation-states. Social scientists have produced much of the work on transnationalism and globalization, often with a presentist orientation. Whether in the examination of social movements, immigration, citizenship, or identity, the massive movement of peoples around the Americas and the communications revolution of the past few decades have both spurred and facilitated this work. For historians, most of the recent work that is styled as transnational has focused on the twentieth century, but important writings have been produced on the nineteenth century as well.

In many ways, an older tradition of intellectual history was an early example of the transnational approach. The many studies of political thought surrounding the wars for independence and nation-building in the nineteenth century clearly demonstrated the truly transatlantic nature of liberalism, nationalism, and republicanism. At the heart of this work was the re-creation of intellectual networks that spanned Europe and the Americas. This early work focused almost entirely on elite figures and tended to emphasize the flow of ideas and cultural influences from Europe westward across the Atlantic. Recent projects have returned to these old subjects, but with an emphasis on the importance of non-elite figures and the innovations of Americans (in the broadest sense of the term) in the creation of novel ideas and cultural influences. In short, they stress that the flows are not unidirectional and that Americans were not simply consumers but also producers of cultural and political innovation.[5]

Historians of immigration have long played a key role in the study of Latin America, from those who studied the movement of Spaniards and Portuguese across the Atlantic, to those studying the forced migration of millions of Africans in the Middle Passage. Many of the more recent publications on migration link up to global networks tying their work to Asia and the Pacific, to the Indian subcontinent, and the Middle East.[6] At times, these historians consciously link to the contemporary world and the origins of Chinese, Japanese, South Asian, and Middle Eastern communities in Latin America today. One of the key features of such works has been a focus on the culture of the sending communities and the cultural negotiations and contestations that take place in the receiving communities.[7] The flow of migrants within the Americas has become a very developed field, with the relationship between Mexico and the United States at the forefront. Histories of the borderlands have helped illustrate the centuries of movement of peoples between areas in what today are Mexico and the United States long before either came into existence.

The cultural turn and efforts to move beyond the nation-state-centered histories of the past have transformed the history of U.S.–Latin American relations. Diplomatic history has a long tradition, and, as seen in chapter 2, it was a staple of early works in the United States. Globalization, post-modernism, the transnational turn, and the end of the Cold War all influenced the move toward international studies that cross political boundaries, but in ways that are very different than traditional diplomatic history and the history of foreign relations. In the United States, two edited collections are emblematic of the shift: *Close Encounters of Empire: Writing the Cultural History of U.S.–Latin American Relations* (1998) and *Imagining Our Americas: Toward a Transnational Frame* (2007). As Gil Joseph points out in his theoretical introduction to the first volume, Latin Americanists have long focused on inter-American relations but tended to privilege diplomacy, economics, and military interventions. Newer work has been concerned with the relationship between culture and power and in destabilizing many traditional categories, such as state, nation, development, and modernity. Much like borderlands history, this new work often adopts the literary concept of "contact zones" (from literary scholar Mary Louise Pratt) to emphasize instability, fluidity, and multiple voices.[8]

U.S. interventions in Central America in the 1980s and then in the Middle East after 2001 spurred historians to produce many fine works on U.S.–Latin American relations during the Cold War and beyond. Greg Grandin has been exceptionally prolific over the past two decades, beginning with a focus on Central America in *The Last Colonial Massacre: Latin America in the Cold War* (2004), then moving to a sweeping assessment of the impact of U.S. interventions in Latin America on the "war on terror" in the Middle East in *Empire's Workshop: Latin America, the United States, and the Rise of the New Imperialism* (2007). Some of the best surveys have been produced by political scientists, such as Lars Schoultz, *Beneath the United States: A History of U.S. Policy Toward Latin America* (1998), and Peter H. Smith, *Talons of the Eagle: Latin America, the United States, and the World* (2011).

While more traditional historical work focused primarily on the nation-state, governments, and official exchanges, the newer transnational work seeks out relationships across borders of scientific institutions, social movements, cultural networks, non-governmental organizations, and many other non-traditional and non-elite actors. Again, much like borderlands history, this new transnational history emerges out of the convergence of scholars in both American studies and Latin American studies seeking to redefine, reconfigure, or dismantle or reconfigure more than half a century of "area studies" work that generally hewed to the political borders of nation-states in the Americas. Some of the most important new research has challenged the notion of "American exceptionalism," recasting the U.S. as an imperial power and reframing the country as a multicultural society with longstanding and powerful contributions from Latin American and Caribbean immigrants. As with the new imperial history in Britain, transnational historians reconstruct and deconstruct notions of gender, race, sexuality, and nationality. Turning away from the older scholarship's focus on nations, the new scholarship challenges "the analytical primacy of the nation, thinking across the Americas."[9]

Studies of music have figured prominently in this transnational shift. Coming out of an American studies background, Micol Seigel's *Uneven Encounters: Making Race and Nation in Brazil and the United States* (2009) strenuously shuns nation-centered analysis to examine relationships and cultural flows between elites and non-elites through coffee consumption, music, and the press as means to understand racial ideas. Coming out of a Latin American history background, Pablo Palomino's *The Invention of Latin American Music* (2020) traces the emergence of the very idea of "Latin American music" through multiple transnational networks over decades. The history of drugs and drug trafficking, by definition, is a prominent transnational story. Paul Gootenberg's *Andean Cocaine: The Making of a Global Drug* (2009) is a good example of a history that spans many political borders while recognizing the importance of them. Public health, medicine, and scientific research have also attracted attention as non-governmental collaborations extending over national boundaries.[10]

A New Economic History?

New approaches to economic history have also spanned national and imperial boundaries in ways that both continue older traditions and break new theoretical ground. With a long tradition of quantification, empiricism, and structures, the economic history of Latin America languished as so many historians took the cultural turn. The dependency theories that had dominated so much of Latin American history, especially in Latin America, beginning in the 1960s built on a tradition of studies of political economy. The cultural turn moved historians away from structures, meta-narratives, and materiality after 1990, especially in the United States. The rise of neo-liberalism and the intensification of globalization moved Latin America into a new phase of economic history as theorists of dependency and world systems receded from the forefront of historical work. (In one striking historical irony, Fernando Henrique Cardoso, one of the most famous theorists of dependency in the 1960s and 1970s, as president of Brazil in the late 1990s implemented a series of profound neo-liberal economic reforms.) With the emergence of formal democracy across most of the region, and the end of revolutionary upheavals, many scholars turned away from economics and development to focus on identities, politics, and culture. Economic history survived, albeit as a very small field on the fringe of the community of Latin American historians in the United States and Europe.

The most vocal advocates of a new economic history looked to U.S. economic theorists for their inspiration, especially Douglass North (1920–2015), winner of the Nobel Prize in Economics along with Robert W. Fogel in 1993. North championed the study of institutions such as property rights, markets, and transaction costs. Stephen Haber (Stanford University and the Hoover Institution) became the most visible advocate for the application of the new institutional economics to Latin American history, as he berated the cultural historians for what he saw as muddled, illogical, and anti-empirical work. The members of the small, but active, group of historians he trained have produced highly sophisticated quantitative analyses of the economic history of Mexico and Brazil, in particular. Unfortunately for the historical profession, economic history has largely been taken over by economists who control the major journals and require a mathematical and theoretical training that few historians choose to follow. Historians of Latin America, especially the less numerate, rarely read this style of economic history, if any at all.[11]

Another, less quantitative and theoretical style of economic history builds on the long tradition in the field focusing on trade and commerce. Most notably, these historians have focused on "commodity chains" following goods across countries, regions, and the globe. This trend somewhat follows the rise of the "new history of capitalism" work that has largely emerged out of U.S. history. This revises the old political economy model to make it less rigid, hierarchical, and deterministic. Publications such as Sven Beckert's *Empire of Cotton* (2014), or Steven Topik's work on coffee, illustrate how particular commodities are produced, circulated, and affect multiple regions of the world. Unlike the old political economy, these historians bring human agency much more prominently into the analysis as they reconstruct networks of people and the creative roles of individuals in the spread of capitalism around the region and the globe. Rather than return to the old-style structuralism and materialism, these historians have examined what might be called the culture of materiality.

The Atlantic World Emerges

Perhaps the most creative and expansive approach that has both revitalized and challenged the field of Latin American history over the past three decades is Atlantic world history. Like the borderlands, it is an approach that has a long history that recent historians have revised and transformed. In a very basic sense, much of the colonial history of Latin America is by its very nature transatlantic, imperial history. The classic works of the Chaunus and Earl Hamilton, in economic history, and the early histories of colonial administration were often topics that spanned the Atlantic Ocean. In the 1970s and 1980s, Bernard Bailyn (1922–2020) at Harvard University and faculty at the Johns Hopkins University developed programs and publication series on Atlantic history. Atlantic world history as a self-conscious and innovative approach begins to emerge full blown in the 1990s and has attracted historians on both sides of the ocean, North and South, although most of the work has been done by historians based in the United States.

At its best, Atlantic world history has forced us to rethink old problems, categories, and connections. At its most mundane, historians of empires, colonization, or specific locales simply claim an Atlantic orientation while going about their work much as historians did before the emergence of this new approach. As Alison Games has pointed out, much of the research has offered up "a history of places around the Atlantic versus a history of the Atlantic."[12] The challenges of writing truly Atlantic-centered history is daunting, given the four continents and thousands of languages, cultures, and polities connected to this immense ocean over multiple centuries. As with borderlands history, the field has attracted critics who question the validity of the conceptualization and boundaries, both spatial and temporal.

Most scholars would probably agree that the Atlantic world begins to take shape in the fifteenth century with European voyages, first down the coast of Africa, with the key moment being the arrival of Columbus in the Caribbean in late 1492. Over several centuries, the movements of peoples across the Atlantic from north to south gradually connected all four continents. More debated is the other end of the timeframe. Most of the work in the field focuses on the colonial era into the nineteenth century. For some, the rise of nation-states between 1776 and the 1830s marks the end of their Atlantic world and the beginning of a more global era. For others, the end of slavery – 1830s in the British Caribbean, 1860s in the United States, and 1880s in Cuba and Brazil – serves as the inflection point. Although some have invoked the terminology for the twentieth century, most working in the field would see the Atlantic world as a historical approach and era stretching from the fifteenth to the nineteenth century.

The best forms of Atlantic world history cross all sorts of boundaries and borders. Much of the work remains bounded by old imperial systems (French, Dutch, British, Spanish, Portuguese) or linguistic expertise. One of the most daunting challenges of Atlantic world history is the task of reading across imperial systems and geographies in multiple languages (an excellent example is Patricia Seed's *Ceremonies of Possession in Europe's Conquest of the New World, 1492–1640* [1995]). Scholars of the Iberoamerican South Atlantic have sometimes criticized their British colleagues for their insularity and tendency to stay within their own imperial (and linguistic) bounds when claiming to write about the Atlantic world. Bernard Bailyn, for example, has been accused of promoting a Eurocentric vision of the field that fails to bring in Africa as a full participant in the analysis.

Leading figures in the field have stressed the need to produce work that is truly transregional and transoceanic, that brings out interconnections, encounters, and exchanges that include multiple ethnicities, cultures, empires, and nations.[13] Much as in cultural history, in general, and borderlands history, in particular, Atlantic world historians stress the agency and contingency of the diverse local peoples, negotiation, contestation, exchange, and hybridity. This last is perhaps the most heavily used concept in cultural history, and Atlantic world history, over the past generation. One of the debates about hybridity that has ensued for decades now is over the term "creolization," its meaning and importance. At its most useful, it refers to the emergence of individuals and cultures out of the mixing (whether through coercion or not) of languages, religious practices, foods, and cultural practices. For some, this has meant the annihilation of cultures (especially of Africans and Native Americans). For others, such as Ira Berlin or Jane Landers, it has been celebrated for its creativity and the agency of individuals moving among multiple empires, nations, ethnicities, and cultures.[14]

Some of the most illuminating, and border crossing, of these studies concentrate on a single commodity – tobacco, cotton, chocolate, wine, sugar, coffee, rice, emeralds, pearls – and trace the networks and pathways from production to consumption. At times, these works come from historians of Africa making their way west to the Americas, at times from historians of British North America stretching into the Caribbean and Atlantic, and sometimes from others whose training is by historians of various parts of the Atlantic world and whose geographic home is not easily circumscribed. The reconstruction of the extensive and circuitous paths of these commodities creates rich and rewarding angles that others have not noticed and appreciated when sticking to imperial or national units. The challenges presented by crossing empires, states, languages, and cultures, however, make the work daunting, especially to break out of boundaries of well-established historiographies.[15]

One of the pioneering areas of Atlantic history, going back decades, has been the study of the transatlantic slave trade. Philip Curtin's magisterial work *The Atlantic Slave Trade: A Census* (1969) was the first rigorous, scholarly attempt to quantify the traffic, and his estimate of 9.5 million Africans transported to the Americas remained a benchmark for decades. High-end estimates are now around 14 to 15 million individuals transported between 1450 and 1870. Curtin (1922–2009) co-founded at the University of Wisconsin in the 1950s one of the first African studies centers and was a driving force in the Atlantic studies program after 1975 at Johns Hopkins. His work on disease, plantations, and trade, *Death by Migration* (1989), *The Rise and Fall of the Plantation Complex* (1990), and *Cross Cultural Trade in World History* (1984), are foundational works in African and Atlantic history. Herbert S. Klein (b. 1936), beginning in the 1960s and continuing into the twenty-first century (with *The Atlantic Slave Trade*, 2010), has further refined and filled out quantitative data on the trade. By the 1990s, the amount of data assembled by various scholars led to the creation of a massive and continually growing database of more than 40,000 voyages of slave ships. Set up by David Eltis (Emory University) and David Richardson (University of Hull), www.slavevoyages.org has become an exceptionally important and useful tool for historians, quantitatively oriented or not. In recent years, historians have also focused greater attention on the internal slave trade within the Americas.

The historiography of the transatlantic slave trade is immense after nearly a half-century of work by historians on four continents. The bulk of this has been done by U.S., British, and Brazilian historians. During the age of social history, many of the studies took a quantitative turn as historians (such as Curtin or Klein) sought to gain an understanding of the magnitude of the commerce, its points of origin and destinations, and the demography of the captive cargo. As historians turned increasingly toward culture, they looked at the diaspora of peoples, languages, and religious systems that human trafficking scattered across the Atlantic world (and beyond). The controversial work of the sociologist Orlando Patterson, *Slavery and Social Death* (1985), Paul Gilroy's pathbreaking *Black Atlantic* (1993), and Lorand Matory's *Black Atlantic Religion* (2005) all probe deeply the social and cultural experiences of Africans on both sides of the Atlantic.

In recent decades, a small but important group of historians has labored to work on both sides of the Atlantic and to recover the African side of the diaspora. John Thornton, Linda Heywood, Joe Miller, Walter Hawthorne, and Mariana

Candido (to name but a few) are fine examples of scholars trained in African history who have looked west across the Atlantic.[16] The vast of majority of the work on Latin America, despite this growing African history grounding, is done by scholars trained in the history of the Americas looking east toward the homelands of the enslaved Africans. Much like borderlands scholars, historians of the Atlantic world are trained in many different types of programs – by historians of Latin America, the Caribbean, the United States, Europe, and Africa. A few universities have brought together faculty working on different geographic regions to create doctoral programs in Atlantic world history (dating back to the 1970s and the Atlantic studies program at Johns Hopkins). The Conference on Latin American History for many years has had committees largely based on national or regional geographies. In the early 2000s, a group of scholars in CLAH created an Atlantic World committee recognizing the burgeoning influence of the field.

Race and Ethnicity

The history of race and ethnicity in Latin America is closely linked to Atlantic world history but certainly has a long tradition of its own. Forged out of the collisions of Native Americans, Africans, and Iberians during three centuries of colonial rule, the histories of race and ethnicity are at the very core of Latin American history. In the past two centuries, migrations of peoples out of the Middle East, South Asia, East Asia, and Europe have contributed to the complex racial and ethnic demography of the region. As with research we have seen on other topics, anthropologists, sociologists, and historians have learned from each other, influenced each other, and even sometimes have collaborated on research to produce innovative work.[17] Over the past century, the ethnographic and theoretical efforts of social scientists have spawned fundamental works that have often spurred historians to seek the origins of contemporary race relations in the past. The classic publications of the Mexican intellectual José Vasconcelos on the "cosmic race," Gilberto Freyre on miscegenation in Brazil, and Caribbean/French/African intellectuals such as Léopold Senghor (1906–2001), Aimé Césaire (1913–2008), and Léon Damas (1912–1978) on *négritude* established a pattern in the early decades of the twentieth century. To understand the history of the region, and of many of the nations in the region, scholars had to come to grips with the history of race and racial thinking.

With the rise of social history, many historians turned to the study of race as an important category of analysis. The impressive expansion of historical work on Afro-Latin Americans and indigenous peoples contributed to the development of race and ethnicity as a growing field. The emergence over centuries of racially and culturally mixed populations in many countries created many intermediate groups who were not black, white, or indigenous. With similar histories of conquest, colonization, slavery, and immigration across the Americas, studies of race and ethnicity often took on a comparative angle. This is most clearly evident in the long tradition of comparative studies of slavery and race relations dating back to at least the 1940s. Carl Degler's multiple prizewinning *Neither Black Nor White* (1971) compared the racial histories of both the U.S. and Brazil in an effort to see how and why race relations took such divergent paths in the two largest slave societies in the Americas. The large *mestizo* or *mulatto* populations in Latin America often played a key role in these national and cross-national studies.

While social history propelled studies of race after 1960, especially from a quantitative angle, the emergence of cultural history unleashed an explosion of theorizing about race, not only in contemporary societies but also back through time. Social scientists and historians emphatically declared race to be a cultural construct, spurring many scholars to research how these racial categories had been constructed and changed over time.[18] In countries such as Guatemala, Peru, Ecuador, and Bolivia, historians often focused on the role of indigenous peoples and how they have been imagined and oppressed.[19] In Mexico and Brazil, two nations that constructed national identities built on racial mixture (*mestizaje, mestiçagem*), some historians examined the ways in which these national narratives became dominant, while others probed the historical construction of the very category of *mestizo/mestiço*.[20] Moving deeper into the colonial past, scholars revealed the incredible complexity and fluidity of categories and the often futile efforts of colonial officials to impose fixed identities on individuals with complicated racial histories.

As studies of contemporary society and historical works have multiplied over the past three decades, the complexity, fluidity, and constructedness of racial and ethnic categories over time have become increasingly clear, even as we debate in our own times the very nature of the categories and who belongs in them. Even when not inspired by or a follower of Foucault, this has led historians to uncover regimes of knowledge about race and ethnicity. Some have done this through intellectual histories of scientists, politicians, and policymakers, while others have delved into the history of institutions that help formalize racial categories such as census bureaus, government agencies, and legal systems.[21] Decades of historical scholarship on race and ethnicity have made it very clear that these are categories that have been culturally and socially constructed in many different ways, at different times, in many societies, but that they have carried (and continue to carry) very real consequences for people as they go about their lives.

A Natural Turn?

Environmental history offers another turn in the historiography over the past generation that sometimes ignores political boundaries within Latin America and, at others, ranges far beyond the region. Although the environment plays an important role in much of the historical scholarship over the last century, approaching the history of Latin America through an environmental lens is a very recent phenomenon.[22] Scholars have produced excellent work on the pre-Columbian and colonial eras, but the field has been dominated by work on post-colonial history, and much of it remains centered on nation-states. It has also been marked by vibrant interdisciplinarity, bringing together experts in the natural sciences, the social sciences, and the humanities.

Geographers, understandably, were early contributors to historical work with an environmental emphasis, most notably those associated with the University of California, Berkeley, in the mid-twentieth century, such as Carl O. Sauer and Robert West. Alfred Crosby (1931–2018) stands out as an important pioneer in the field, with his pathbreaking achievements *The Columbian Exchange* (1972) and *Ecological Imperialism* (1986). Crosby's work boldly set out the importance of the global transformation ignited by the ongoing and irreversible process Columbus initiated in 1492 – the profound impact of the exchange of germs, plants, animals, and humans. *The Columbian Exchange* is a work that vividly demonstrates the "biological and cultural consequences of 1492" by continually ignoring political boundaries, of both nations and empires. His study of "ecological imperialism" focuses on how the Europeans sought to create neo-Europes around the globe, producing ecological devastation in their path.

A great deal of the work on environmental history recounts the devastation of Latin America through deforestation, disease, mining, and large-scale agricultural transformation. Another of the pioneers in the field, Warren Dean (1932–1994), moved from studying industrialization in São Paulo to the coffee economy in the countryside, and then to full-fledged environmental history. In *Brazil and the Struggle for Rubber* (1987) he recast our understanding of the Amazonian rubber boom in the late nineteenth century by showing how South American leaf blight made plantation rubber production impossible in Brazil. A fungus found in nature changed the course of Brazilian and world history. Dean's final work, *With Broadax and Firebrand* (1995), is a passionate analysis of the "destruction of the Brazilian Atlantic forest" over five centuries of human occupation and exploitation.

As Crosby demonstrated, the introduction of new plants and animals transformed the ecology of the Americas. Elinor Melville's outstanding *A Plague of Sheep* (1994) (originally a dissertation produced under the guidance of Charles Gibson) is a pioneering analysis of the relationship between new fauna and American landscapes. The biological and botanical exchanges between the Americas and other regions of the globe have been the focus of a number of excellent works over the past two decades. Much as in Atlantic world or borderlands history, these works cross many borders and have been written by historians who sometimes see themselves as Latin American specialists but also include those trained in U.S., Caribbean, European, and African history.[23]

Even before the recent emergence of environmental history, the relationship between human society and nature played a role in many studies, especially those looking at the exploitation of the land. Many of the early works on colonial silver production included research on the environmental impact of mining and refining, especially deforestation, mercury poisoning, and water pollution. Truly environmental histories of mining date from very recent decades, and much of this work has concentrated on the post-colonial period.[24] One of the areas with the most vibrant work has been plantation agriculture, especially for the modern period. Recent studies on bananas in Central America, henequen in the Yucatan, and sugar in Brazil are but three examples that link up the history of agri-business, ecology, and politics in creative ways. Myrna Santiago's book on the ecology of oil in early twentieth-century Mexico is an excellent example of the environmental turn applied to industries that have been well studied from other angles. As with so many of the other recent publications we have seen, these works often move across multiple political and geographic units.[25] Greg Cushman's *Guano and the Opening of the Pacific World* (2013) uses the tiny islands off the Peruvian coast as the anchor for an analysis that moves across most of the Pacific Ocean and beyond.

Along with devastation, conservation has been a major theme in recent works on environmental history. Most of this has been on the twentieth century. Emily Wakild and Lane Simonian's books look at conservation in Mexico, while Sterling Evans's *Green Republic* (1999) is a critical examination of Costa Rica's history of the conservation, and destruction, of its famous forests.[26] One of the most dynamic areas of research in recent years has concerned efforts to control and allocate water resources, especially in Mexico, during both the colonial and post-colonial eras.[27] Climate and climate change have also become an important focus of research. Scholars have written about hurricanes in the Atlantic, melting glaciers in the Andes, and El Niño.[28]

Much as in borderlands history, historians have produced an array of work across countries and many types of environments, but there are far more case studies than syntheses. The historical overviews of the region (so far) have generally taken on a set of themes or concentrated on either the colonial or the post-colonial period.[29] A sure sign of the development of the field is the creation of the Latin American and Caribbean Society of Environmental History (La Sociedad Latinoamericana y Caribeña de Historia Ambiental, SOLCHA) in 2004, with its own conference every other year (www.solcha.org). The lively debates among this growing group of historians is another sign of the coming of age of the field as they learn from the work of historians in other regions of the globe and engage in self-critiques. At the forefront of such debates is the very nature of nature itself. The cultural turn in U.S. and European environmental history has led some to argue that nature is a cultural construct and that environmental historians must break down the barriers between the human and the natural that characterizes the approach of many historians. The move to put the non-human (especially plants and animals) into more active roles in history challenges more traditional environmental history and the very nature of history itself.[30]

Science, Medicine, Public Health, and Technology

At times closely linked to environmental history, but with much longer and developed traditions of their own, are the histories of science, medicine, and public health in Latin America. Early works dating back to the beginning of the twentieth century, especially in Argentina and Mexico, generally celebrated heroic figures and achievements in an area of the world often seen by those in the North Atlantic as lacking a tradition in modern science and medicine. The classic early publications of José Babini, *La evolución del pensamiento científico argentino* (1954), and Eli de Gortari, *La ciencia en la historia de México* (1963), reflect a traditional historiographical approach. Until late in the century, historians of science and medicine in Europe and the United States generally viewed modernity and science as originating and diffusing outward from Europe. The traditional historiography depicted Spain and Portugal, and hence their colonies, as missing the Scientific Revolution and hindered by Catholic values and culture. In the 1970s and 1980s, graduate programs in Latin America and the United States began to produce historians of science, medicine, and technology who have created a vibrant transatlantic community built on many strong national groups of historians. Their work has been marked at times both by strong nationalism and, in some studies, by a truly transatlantic and even global approach.[31]

Much of the growing body of work after 1960 reflected the influence of modernization and dependency theories. The predominant model in the history of science in the North Atlantic world viewed "modern science" as a Western creation that gradually diffused to other areas of the globe. Many of the early scholars studying science, medicine, and technology, either as historians or as scientists and social scientists, sought to understand the weaknesses of science on the "periphery" to build national scientific and technical infrastructures for the development of their nations. Some of the early scholarly studies focused on the development (and underdevelopment) of scientific institutions and communities. Nancy Stepan's *Beginnings of Brazilian Science* (1976) is a landmark work in a field that was just emerging, and the beginning of a long and productive career.[32] Much of the early research also focused on the role of science in the building of nations and national institutions.

Early work also tended to emphasize the unidirectional flow of ideas, imperialism, colonialism, and scientific knowledge. The influence of cultural history, post-colonialism, and Bourdieu moved historians toward a "hybrid" or "creole" vision of science, technology, and medicine in Latin America. By the 1990s and early 2000s, cutting-edge work emphasized the intellectual and cultural exchanges among foreign scientists and locals. Neil Safier's *Measuring the New World* (2008), for example, reexamines an eighteenth-century Franco-Spanish expedition to South America to determine the shape of the Earth. Rather than focus on the European scientific contribution to Latin America, Safier shows the flow of knowledge from West to East through the contributions of locals (including the indigenous and Afrodescendants) to the formation of scientific knowledge. The study of scientific expeditions in the colonial era has a long tradition, but those published in recent decades, such as Safier, uncover the ground-level, social and cultural exchanges between actors in what used to be called the periphery and the center.[33]

Historians of science and medicine have been at the forefront of this cultural and intellectual revisionism, decentering old Eurocentric narratives. They have shown that Latin America in the colonial period was not a scientific and intellectual wasteland devoid of knowledge about the latest research or barren of originality. The work of Stuart Schwartz on the Inquisition and Jorge Cañizares-Esguerra on science attempt to upend traditional versions of the early modern Atlantic world. Both make convincing arguments for Iberian and Iberoamerican contributions to the emergence of modern science, religious toleration, and the Enlightenment.[34] Recent works have deconstructed once stable categories – science, tropics, tropical medicine, nature – emphasizing the cultural constructions of Europeans as they moved around Latin America and the globe encountering new peoples, flora, fauna, and geographies. Many of these studies continue to focus on nations in the nineteenth and twentieth centuries. The most innovative and provocative among them turn to the colonial era and the fascinating mix of cultures and peoples producing "alternative epistemologies" and knowledges that eventually become labeled science, medicine, or witchcraft, shamanism, and popular healing.[35]

Many of the studies that appeared in the 1970s and 1980s about the role of foreign actors and institutions on science, medicine, and public health in Latin America reflected the influence of dependency theory. These often stressed the ways foreign scientists or institutions such as the Rockefeller Foundation manipulated or exploited local conditions. Over the last two decades, historians have continued to show the power of the external actor, but now with much greater attention to local agency and the interaction of domestic actors and agencies with external ones. Rather than see foreign scientists working and living in Latin America as agents of imperialism or colonialism, historians now tend to view them as mediating figures in an imperial or transnational landscape.[36] In general, Latin American scholars have emphasized "mediation and reinterpretation" and "a bi-directional movement that involves negotiations and accommodations in center–periphery relations."[37] More recent work has also, to use the phrase of Marcos Cueto, sought out "scientific excellence on the periphery."[38]

The history of disease has been one of the most dynamic areas of research in recent decades. Alfred Crosby's classic work on the microbial exchange drew on an already long tradition in the field, especially the classic work of the Berkeley School, dating back to the 1950s, on the demographic collapse of Native American populations. The quantitative turn in the 1960s and 1970s built on this pioneering research. Much of the work on disease over the last quarter-century has taken this quantitative work as its foundation, though placing a greater emphasis on the cultural and social consequences of disease. While work has continued on the colonial era, a rich literature has emerged on many different types of diseases and epidemics, such as tuberculosis and AIDS.[39]

Often closely linked to the history of disease, public health has attracted the attention of a strong community of historians and social scientists across Latin America, most notably in Brazil. The Oswaldo Cruz Foundation (which served as the focus of Nancy Stepan's first book) became the country's premier public health research institute and developed an outstanding program in the history of science and medicine in the late twentieth century with its own first-rate journal. The work on the history of public health has become a truly interdisciplinary field and one that also often connects directly to contemporary issues. Although many of the studies focus on national institutions, the work is increasingly transnational and global in its approach.[40]

Influenced by the cultural turn, historians of post-colonial Latin America have generated an innovative body of work on race, eugenics, nation-building, and empire. Here, again, Nancy Stepan was a pioneer. *The Hour of Eugenics* (1991) revealed the many creative ways Latin American thinkers adapted and refashioned eugenics to the specific racial and gender dynamics in their own nations. Foucault's concept of bio-power, of disciplining populations through schools, militaries, and hospitals, has greatly influenced many of these studies. Once again, rather than seeing Latin Americans as simply passive consumers of European and U.S. science and technology, recent work has emphasized the creativity and originality of scientists, public health officials, and intellectuals.[41] The turn to health has generated many publications on women and gender. Some concentrate on an analysis of discourse, others on politics and policy. As with race, historians have deconstructed gendered notions of national identity and nation formation. Maternalism, maternity, childbearing, and prostitution have emerged as key themes in recent decades, along with the history of the body.[42]

Linked to the emergence of the history of science and medicine is the history of technology. Much less developed, the field has attracted few historians and a somewhat more substantial group of social scientists. An essential piece of what is usually called science and technology studies (STS), the history of technology has not really emerged as a distinct field, yet. While historians of science have produced some synthetic works over the past few decades, the presence of scholars studying Latin America is rare at the Society for the History of Technology (SHOT). Notably, when historians of science in Latin America organized their own professional organization (1982), they included the history of technology (Sociedad Latinoamericana de Historia de las Ciencias y la Tecnología). The organization and its journal, *Quipu*, have been run overwhelmingly by historians of science.[43] Historians have produced some outstanding work on the history of technology in Latin America, but rarely do they see themselves as historians of technology.[44]

Unity and Diversity

For the past thirty years, historians of Latin America have produced an expanding body of work enriched through the use of very diverse source materials and innovative methodological approaches, and by shifting the very dimensions and definitions of the region they study. Atlantic world history, borderlands history, transnational studies – to name the most obvious – have generated fascinating scholarship while also challenging the very notion of Latin American history. The first two approaches draw on longstanding and strong connections to work in a field more traditionally labeled "colonial Latin America," such as the processes of conquest, colonization, and economic and social structures. At the same time, they reorient the gaze of the historian away from Latin America to new geographies and conceptual units. They implicitly (and sometimes explicitly) question the conceptual category that for so long has so imperfectly defined the field of Latin American history. In the Epilogue, I return to where this book began, with the concept of Latin America, its past, and its future.

Epilogue: The Future of Latin American History

Is there a future for Latin American history? As the previous chapters have shown, the field certainly has a long and rich history, beginning with the works of the colonizers and the colonized and then coming of age in the nineteenth century, largely out of the nation-building projects in the aftermath of the wars for independence. The works of gentlemen scholars in the nineteenth century in the U.S., Europe, and Latin America forged the outlines of historical work that initially read the history of nations back into the colonial and, at times, pre-Columbian past. By the dawn of the twentieth century, academic historians in universities began to appear, and by mid-century they had reached a critical mass in the United States and several Latin American countries. Postwar economic expansion, the Cuban Revolution, and the geopolitics of the Cold War produced a boom in Latin American studies in the 1960s in the U.S. and the U.K. Amid revolutionary movements, the rise of authoritarian regimes, and a burgeoning population, many Latin American universities expanded and produced ever larger numbers of academic historians in the last decades of the twentieth century.

Yet, the very success of the field in producing outstanding scholarship and many brilliant scholars stimulated a self-critique of the idea of Latin America, an idea that appeared fitfully in the mid-nineteenth century and came fully of age in the second half of the twentieth. In the early twentieth century, scholars in North America worked to create a professional community of historians of Latin America. By the beginning of the twenty-first century, some very influential voices within the academic community made serious and sustained arguments against the very existence of Latin America and questioned the basis for a community of specialists around the idea of a region called Latin America. In the words of Walter Mignolo, one of the most vocal critics of seeing Latin America as a region, "Latin America is now the perspective, not the area of study."[1] Clearly, almost no one finds the term "Latin" America satisfactory, even those who argue that there is some conceptual logic and historical rationale for this badly named region. The Mexican historian Mauricio Tenorio-Trillo, who has made his academic career in the United States for decades, after spending more than 150 pages in a sustained critique of the term, admits defeat and declares that it "will endure for the foreseeable future."[2]

The movements within the profession toward the study of borderlands, the Atlantic world, the transnational, and global history have produced innovative work on Latin America while implicitly (and sometimes explicitly) challenging the viability of continuing to envision the region as a coherent and intellectually defensible idea. Many of the intellectuals who birthed the idea defined Latin America in opposition to the emerging power of the United States in the nineteenth century. The emergence of the United States on the world stage after 1898 gave Latin Americans even more cause to draw the contrast and historians in the north to coalesce around a definition of what they saw as a distinct region to the south. The geopolitics of the Cold War motivated the financial and bureaucratic power of the United States government, foundations, and universities to consecrate the regional terminology. Ironically, this peak moment of power in the "American Century" also evoked a sense of solidarity and greater support for the idea among the peoples of the region.

Nearing the end of the first quarter of the twenty-first century, the shifting *historical* conjuncture likely marks the transition to a new *historiographical* conjuncture. The European cultural and economic influences (especially British and French) that defined Latin America in the nineteenth century seem far away and long ago with the demise of the British empire and the rise of multiple global cultural centers. The American Century is over, especially in Latin America, and the Asian Century is well underway as China has become the major economic partner of Brazil, Chile, and other Latin American nations. China's rising power in the region will likely continue, as will the declining influence of the United States. This is truly a regional and global shift at least as important as the 1930s and the 1820s. China may well be preparing its own cadres of "area studies specialists" as it expands its power and influence around the globe, but, so far, it has not had any significant impact on the production and development in the field of Latin American history. Its impact on the region – so far – is largely geopolitical and economic.

The academic communities on three continents reflect the shifting global power dynamics. The community of historians in continental Europe and the United Kingdom remains small but vibrant. In the United States and Canada, the number of historians of Latin America has hovered at over 1,000 for several decades. More than 80 percent of U.S. history departments now include a historian of Latin America. In Latin America, the numbers vary enormously by country. Mexico and Brazil, with more than half the population of Latin America, are home to probably 8,000 to 10,000 historians, most of whom study their own country's history. Some two hundred years after the wars for independence that gave rise to most of the nations traditionally considered part of Latin America, the historical community of those whose work focuses on areas of the Americas that once were, or now are considered, part of Latin America is substantial. In the coming decades, there will be no shortage of historians who work on the former. The question is: will they consider themselves historians of Latin America?

In broad strokes, social history dominated from the 1960s to the 1980s and cultural history from the late 1980s to the early 2000s, even as many other approaches emerged and generated excellent work. Are we in the midst of another cyclical historiographical shift? Are we seeing the emergence of a cultural history that draws on the social, which will lead to a blending of work that is grounded in both the sociological and the cultural approach? Wherever the broad trend leads, we will certainly continue to see outstanding and innovative research on slavery, indigenous peoples, race, the environment, science, medicine, and gender (to name just a few topics). The kind of work produced, as always, will depend on the structural conditions that shape the formation of the next generations of historians.

From the long-term view of the historian, the 1820s was a decade of war and nation-building in much of Latin America. The 1920s in Europe and the Americas was a decade of recovery from the first global war and, in much of the Americas, a period of economic expansion on the eve of a Great Depression. At the beginning of the 2020s, we face enormous uncertainties in a world that has inescapably and irrevocably become globalized, interconnected by trade, migration, and digital media. The shrinking of the globe has facilitated historical research, collaboration, and the dissemination of historical work on a scale and scope and at a speed that is unprecedented. Yet, the historical moment is one of economic and political crises and a reshaping of universities that presents challenges to the work of all historians.

Universities in Europe and the Americas face a serious restructuring that will sorely test the future and relevance of history and the humanities. The number of academic positions in history will likely shrink in the coming decades, and job security will become more tenuous. The pressure to "produce" has been escalating for at least two decades and will continue. This will be a further stimulus to specialization, on the one hand, and collaboration on the other. Larger, more sweeping, projects will likely emerge out of the collaboration of specialists, across disciplines and political borders. Events over the last two decades in the European Union and the United Kingdom may be a foreshadowing of the future for historians in the United States and Latin America. The story of the modern research university over the last half-century has been the accelerating pursuit of more and more funds – from governments, foundations, and donors. As in the past, this will push historians to conceive of research projects that can fit the grant priorities of funding sources, and it will shape the directions of their careers.

Powerful institutional pressures have already moved historians to reconceptualize their teaching, especially the long

Epilogue: The Future of Latin American History

tradition of dividing the world up into geographical and political units and time periods that have privileged the "rise of the West" and the nation-state. In the United Kingdom and the United States this has meant a greater emphasis on themes and issues across political boundaries. In a strange sort of way, the larger intellectual and institutional forces in the profession may have moved historians of Latin America increasingly to bridge boundaries and borders, to fit the region into the larger global context, and to move away from concentrating on a regional orientation.

As this brief survey of the history of Latin American history shows, the field has been enriched over many decades through the interactions of scholars from many countries and regions and across many disciplines and methodologies. Indeed, this has been true for Latin American studies in general. The willingness of so many scholars to look beyond the historical discipline, to anthropology, cultural studies, economics, political science, and sociology (to cite the most obvious), reveals their desire to understand and interpret the past. Long before interdisciplinarity became a buzzword in academia, historians of Latin America were frequently crossing disciplinary boundaries seeking to comprehend the region. Let us hope that this long tradition continues to enrich the field in an age of globalization and professional specialization.

For more than a century, professional historians on three continents have conceptualized and written about a region they have called Latin America. At the core of that idea was the argument that areas of the Americas once stretching from western North America to Patagonia had a common history. The Spanish and Portuguese monarchies invaded, conquered, colonized, and extended their (often tenuous) administration over these lands beginning in the late fifteenth century. For more than three centuries, especially in the core regions of Mesoamerica, the Andes, Brazil, and the Caribbean, the Iberian empires sought to impose their religion, language, culture, political control, and economic systems as Native Americans, enslaved Africans, and their descendants resisted and struggled to retain as much as they could of their collapsing worlds. The three great rivers of peoples collided across the Americas beginning in the late fifteenth century, and the resulting collision of cultures created something new and dynamic out of this mixing of peoples.

If there is something we can call (however badly named) Latin America, it is forged in these collisions like a great new river created out of the confluence of three teeming streams of humanity. Yet, even for those most attached to the idea of Latin America, it is clear that the great river had already begun to split into many separate streams by 1800, much as the Amazon fragments into many rivers as it nears the equatorial Atlantic. As the region entered the twentieth century, the many paths had diverged even more, and the commonalities forged in the colonial crucible faded. By the first decades of the twenty-first century, the growing differences make it increasingly difficult to see the nineteen or twenty nations traditionally associated with Latin America as a coherent regional unit. With diminishing U.S. power in the region, varying levels of integration with the U.S., the European Union, and China, the pronounced social, cultural, and economic differences within the region stand out. Even the Iberian cultural ethos that elites of the region shared for centuries now gradually slips into the past in a world of accelerating cultural influences from all parts of the globe. If there ever was a common colonial heritage, is its hold on this vast region as shared as we once imagined? Do Brazil and Mexico today really have that much in common with, say, Nicaragua and Cuba? Have the various parts of Latin America become so diverse economically and culturally that the commonalities of the colonial era recede in importance?

Scholars will continue to debate the meaning and validity of the idea of Latin America to describe the past of a region where Spain and Portugal once attempted to rule over nearly all South America, the Caribbean, Central America, and Mexico. The continuing divergence of the many parts of the old Iberian empires in the Americas, however, will make it increasingly difficult in the coming years to argue for the continuing coherence of a regional identity. Latin America may have a common past, but it may not have a common future.

Notes

Chapter 1 What Is Latin America?

1 See, for example, J. H. Elliott, *The Old World and the New, 1492–1650* (New York: Cambridge University Press, 1970).
2 Thomas H. Holloway, "Introduction," in Thomas H. Holloway, ed., *A Companion to Latin American History* (Malden, MA: Wiley-Blackwell, 2011), pp. 1–9; Michel Gobat, "The Invention of Latin America: A Transnational History of Anti-Imperialism, Democracy, and Race," *American Historical Review*, 118/5 (2013): 1345–75.
3 For an important discussion of this topic, see Mark T. Berger, *Under Northern Eyes: Latin American Studies and U.S. Hegemony in the Americas, 1898–1990* (Bloomington: Indiana University Press, 1995), esp. pp. 16–17. See also Richard D. Lambert, et al., ed., *Beyond Growth: The Next Stages in Language and Area Studies* (Washington, DC: Association of American Universities, 1984); David Szanton, ed., *The Politics of Knowledge: Area Studies and the Disciplines* (Berkeley: University of California Press, 2004), esp. Paul W. Drake and Lisa Hilbink, "Latin American Studies: Theory and Practice," pp. 34–73; Helen Delpar, *Looking South: The Evolution of Latin Americanist Scholarship in the United States, 1850–1975* (Tuscaloosa: University of Alabama Press, 2008); Ricardo Donato Salvatore, *Disciplinary Conquest: U.S. Scholars in South America, 1900–1945* (Durham, NC: Duke University Press, 2016).
4 José Moya, "Introduction," in José Moya, ed., *The Oxford*

Handbook of Latin American History (New York: Oxford University Press, 2010), p. 18.

5 For a fascinating analysis of the "invention" of world regions, see Martin W. Lewis and Kären E. Wigen, *The Myth of Continents: A Critique of Metageography* (Berkeley: University of California Press, 1997), esp. pp. 162–82. The U.S. Department of Education defines Latin American Studies as "A program that focuses on the history, society, politics, culture, and economics of one or more of the Hispanic peoples of the North and South American Continents outside Canada and the United States, including the study of the Pre-Columbian period and the flow of immigrants from other societies" (http://nces.ed.gov/ipeds/cipcode/cipdetail.aspx?y=55&cipid=88024).

6 Walter D. Mignolo, *The Idea of Latin America* (Malden, MA: Blackwell, 2005).

7 William Spence Robertson, *Rise of the Spanish-American Republics as Told in the Lives of Their Liberators* (New York: D. Appleton & Co., 1921); Herman G. James and Percy A. Martin, *The Republics of Latin America: Their History, Governments and Economic Conditions* (New York: Harper & Brothers, 1923); Hubert Herring, *A History of Latin America from the Beginnings to the Present* (3rd edn, New York: Knopf, 1968); John Gunther, *Inside Latin America* (New York: Harper & Brothers, 1941).

8 Dana Gardner Munro, *The Latin American Republics: A History* (New York: Appleton-Century-Crofts, 1942); J. Fred Rippy, *Latin America: A Modern History* (Ann Arbor: University of Michigan Press, 1958); Edward Gaylord Bourne, *Spain in America, 1450–1580* (New York: Harper & Brothers, 1904); Charles Edward Chapman, *Colonial Hispanic America: A History* (New York: Macmillan, 1933); John A. Crow, *The Epic of Latin America* (4th edn, Berkeley: University of California Press, 1992 [originally pubd by Doubleday (1946)]; Donald E. Worcester and Wendell G. Schaeffer, *The Growth and Culture of Latin America* (New York: Oxford University Press, 1956).

9 E. Bradford Burns, *Latin America: A Concise Interpretive History* (6th edn, Englewood Cliffs, NJ: Prentice-Hall, 1994).

10 The first edition of Keen's book appeared in 1980 as *A Short History of Latin America* (Boston: Houghton Mifflin), with Mark Wasserman as the co-author. Wasserman had dropped off the title page by the fourth edition (1992), and the sixth and seventh editions, *A History of Latin America* (2000 and 2004), are co-authored with Keith Haynes. John Charles Chasteen, *Born in Blood and Fire: A Concise History of Latin America*

(New York: W. W. Norton, 2001); Lawrence A. Clayton and Michael L. Conniff, *A History of Modern Latin America* (Fort Worth: Harcourt Brace, 1999); Thomas E. Skidmore and Peter H. Smith, *Modern Latin America* (2nd edn, New York: Oxford University Press, 1989); Edwin Williamson, *The Penguin History of Latin America* (London: Penguin, 1992).

11 Leslie Bethell, ed., *The Cambridge History of Latin America*, Vol. I: *Colonial Latin America* (Cambridge: Cambridge University Press, 1984), p. xiv.

Chapter 2 The Pioneering Generations

1 Bartolomé de las Casas, *Historia de las Indias*, 3 vols, was composed between 1527 and 1561. Although there are many versions in Spanish, the complete work has never been translated into English.
2 *Hernán Cortés: Letters from Mexico*, trans. and ed. Anthony Pagden (New Haven, CT: Yale University Press, 1986); Miguel León-Portilla, ed., *The Broken Spears: The Aztec Account of the Conquest of Mexico* (Boston: Beacon Press, 1962).
3 Benjamin Keen, "Main Currents in United States Writings on Colonial Spanish America, 1884–1984," *Hispanic American Historical Review*, 65/4 (1985): 657–82, at p. 658.
4 See, for example, Rebecca Earle, *The Return of the Native: Indians and Myth-Making in Spanish America, 1810–1930* (Durham, NC: Duke University Press, 2007).
5 Keen, "Main Currents," p. 660.
6 Bernard Moses, *The Spanish Dependencies in South America: An Introduction to the History of Their Civilization* (New York: Harper & Brothers, 1914), *The Establishment of Spanish Rule in South America: An Introduction to the History and Politics of Spanish America* (New York: G. P. Putnam's Sons, 1898); and Edward Gaylord Bourne, *Spain in America, 1450–1580* (New York: Harper & Brothers, 1904).
7 Keen, "Main Currents," p. 664.
8 William Spence Robertson, *Hispanic American Relations with the United States*, ed. David Kinley (New York: Oxford University Press, 1928); Dexter Perkins, *The Monroe Doctrine, 1826–1867* (Baltimore: Johns Hopkins University Press, 1933); Arthur P. Whitaker, *The United States and the Independence of Latin America, 1800–1830* (New York: Russell & Russell, 1941).
9 Guillermo Zermeño Padilla, "Mexican Historical Writing," in Axel Schneider and Daniel Woolf, eds, *The Oxford History of*

Historical Writing, Vol. 5: *Historical Writing since 1945* (New York: Oxford University Press, 2011), p. 457.

10 Tulio Halperín Donghi, *Testimonio de un observador participante: medio siglo de estudios latinoamericanos en un mundo cambiante* (Buenos Aires: Prometeo Libros, 2013).

11 Gabriel Paquette, "The 'Parry Report' (1965) and the Establishment of Latin American Studies in the United Kingdom," *Historical Journal*, 62/1 (2019): 219–40, at p. 228.

12 Robin Humphreys, *British Consular Reports on the Trade and Politics of Latin America, 1824–1826* (London: Royal Historical Society, 1940); John Lynch, *Latin American Revolutions, 1808–1826* (New York: W. W. Norton, 1973); John H. Elliott, *Imperial Spain, 1469–1716* (London: Edward Arnold, 1963).

13 Alexander Marchant, *From Barter to Slavery: The Economic Relations of Portuguese and Indians in the Settlement of Brazil, 1500–1580* (Gloucester, MA: Peter Lang, 1966). The quote is from p. 77. The first monograph, Alan K. Manchester, *British Preeminence in Brazil: Its Rise and Decline* (Chapel Hill: University of North Carolina Press, 1933), was also essentially a study of European influence in Brazil.

14 Richard M. Morse, *New World Soundings: Culture and Ideology in the Americas* (Baltimore: Johns Hopkins University Press, 1989); *O espelho de Próspero: cultura e idéias nas Américas*, trans. Paulo Neves (São Paulo: Companhia das Letras, 1988); Lewis Hanke, *Bartolomé de las Casas: An Interpretation of His Life and Writings* (The Hague: Martinus Nijhoff, 1951); John Tate Lanning, *The Eighteenth-Century Enlightenment in the University of San Carlos de Guatemala* (Ithaca, NY: Cornell University Press, 1956).

15 Quoted in Charles Gibson and Benjamin Keen, "Trends of United States Studies in Latin American History," *American Historical Review*, 62/4 (1957): 855–77, at p. 865.

16 Frank Tannenbaum, *Mexico: The Struggle for Peace and Bread* (New York: Alfred A. Knopf, 1950); Howard Cline, *The United States and Mexico* (Cambridge, MA: Harvard University Press, 1953); Charles Curtis Cumberland, *Mexican Revolution: Genesis under Madero* (Austin: University of Texas Press, 1952); Stanley R. Ross, *Francisco I. Madero: Apostle of Mexican Democracy* (New York: Columbia University Press, 1955).

17 Both the distribution of scholars and their regional interests within the Conference on Latin American History provide a fair indication of the dominance of Mexico. Of the approximately 1,300 CLAH members in 2020, some 350 belong to the

Notes to pp. 33–40   131

Mexican Studies Section, roughly twice the size of the Andean Studies or the Brazilian Studies Section.
18 Sherburne F. Cook and Lesley Byrd Simpson, *The Population of Central Mexico in the Sixteenth Century* (Berkeley: University of California Press, 1948); Borah and Cook's most important work in this period is *The Aboriginal Population of Central Mexico on the Eve of the Spanish Conquest* (Berkeley: University of California Press, 1963).
19 Charles Gibson, *The Aztecs under Spanish Rule: A History of the Indians of the Valley of Mexico in the Sixteenth Century* (Stanford, CA: Stanford University Press, 1964).
20 Howard F. Cline, comp. and ed., *Latin American History: Essays on Its Study and Teaching, 1898–1965*, 2 vols (Austin: University of Texas Press, 1967), and *National Directory of Latin Americanists: Bibliographies of 1,844 Specialists in the Social Sciences and Humanities* (Washington, DC: Hispanic Foundation Bibliographical Series No. 10, Government Printing Office, 1966).

Chapter 3 The Economic and Quantitative Turns

1 Richard D. Lambert, ed., *Beyond Growth: The Next Stage in Language and Area Studies* (Washington, DC: Association of American Universities, 1984), p. 9.
2 Robert B. Townsend, "Precedents: The Job Crisis of the 1970s," *AHA Perspectives*, 35/4 (1997): 9–13; and "Job Report 1997: Bleak Outlook for the History Job Market," ibid.: 7–11.
3 In the early 1990s, for example, the average number of positions in Latin American history advertised in the *AHA Perspectives* was thirty-four, with more than eighty applicants for each. According to *Dissertation Abstracts*, the average number of new Ph.D.s in the early 1990s was around fifty per year. Robert B. Townsend, "Studies Report Mixed News for History Job Seekers," *AHA Perspectives*, 35/3 (1997): 8. In 1992, "American universities produced 725 new history Ph.D.s; of these, 34.2 percent were women." Carla Hesse, "Report on the Status and Hiring of Women and Minority Historians in Academia," *AHA Perspectives*, 34/3 (1996): 35.
4 Noble David Cook, *Demographic Collapse: Indian Peru, 1520–1620* (New York: Cambridge University Press, 1981); Robert McCaa, *Marriage and Fertility in Chile: Demographic Turning Points in the Petorca Valley, 1840–1976* (Boulder, CO: Westview Press, 1983); Henry F. Dobyns, "Estimating Aboriginal American Population: An Appraisal of Techniques

with a New Hemispheric Estimate," *Current Anthropology*, 7/4 (1966): 395; Linda Newson, *The Cost of Conquest: Indian Decline in Honduras under the Spanish Rule* (Boulder, CO: Westview Press, 1986), and *Indian Survival in Colonial Nicaragua* (Norman: University of Oklahoma Press, 1987). For a very bitter and sustained attack on much of this demographic work, see David Henige, *Numbers from Nowhere: The American Indian Contact Population Debate* (Norman: University of Oklahoma Press, 1998).

5 Robert William Fogel and Stanley L. Engerman, *Time on the Cross: The Economics of American Negro Slavery* (Boston: Little, Brown, 1974). Fogel and Engerman published a second volume that offered colleagues the data and methods of the interpretations. *Time on The Cross: Evidence and Methods – A Supplement* (Boston: Little, Brown, 1974).

6 See the special issue "Mexico's New Cultural History: una lucha libre?" *Hispanic American Historical Review*, 79/2 (1999), especially Stephen Haber, "Anything Goes: Mexico's 'New' Cultural History," pp. 309–30.

7 Considered a classic work of the twentieth century, Lévi-Strauss's memoir draws extensively on his fieldwork in Brazil: *Tristes Tropiques* (Paris: Librarie Plon, 1955); *Tristes Tropiques*, trans. John Weightman and Doreen Weightman (New York: Atheneum, 1973).

8 Pierre Chaunu, *Structures et conjoncture de l'Atlantique espagnol et hispano-américain (1504–1650)*, 3 vols (Paris: Institut des hautes études de l'Amérique Latine, 1959); Enrique Florescano, *Precios del maíz y crisis agrícolas en México (1708–1810): ensayo sobre el movimiento de los precios y sus consecuencias económicas y sociales* (Mexico City: Colegio de México, 1969); Maria Bárbara Levy, *História da bolsa de valores do Rio de Janeiro* (Rio de Janeiro: IBMEC, 1977); Maria Luiza Marcilio, *A cidade de São Paulo: povoamento e população, 1750–1850* (São Paulo: Livraria Pioneira, Editora da Universidade de São Paulo, 1974); Frédéric Mauro, *Le Portugal et l'Atlantique au XVIIe siècle, 1570–1670: étude économique* (Paris: S.E.V.P.E.N., 1960); Ciro F. S. Cardoso and Héctor Pérez-Brignoli, *Los métodos de la historia: introducción a los problemas, métodos y técnicas de la historia demográfica, económica y social* (Mexico City: Editorial Grijalba, 1977).

9 José Carlos Mariátegui, *Seven Interpretive Essays on Peruvian Reality*, trans. Marjory Urquidi (Austin: University of Texas Press, 1971 [originally pubd in Spanish in 1928]); Caio Prado Junior, *The Colonial Background of Modern Brazil*, trans. Suzette Macedo (Berkeley: University of California Press,

1967), originally pubd as *Formação econômica do Brasil contemporâneo* (São Paulo: Livraria Martins Editora, 1942); Julio César Jobet, *Los fundamentos del marxismo* (4th edn, Santiago: Prensa Latinoamericana, 1964 [1st edn, 1939]).

10 The term was first used by the French geographer Alfred Sauvy: "Trois mondes, une planète," *L'Observateur*, 118 (14 August 1952), p. 14.

11 Fernando Henrique Cardoso and Enzo Faletto, *Dependencia y desarrollo en América Latina* (Mexico City: Siglo Veintiuno, 1969); *Dependency and Development in Latin America*, trans. Marjory Mattingly Urquidi (Berkeley: University of California Press, 1979).

12 For a discussion of this literature, see William Ryan Wishart, "Underdeveloping Appalachia: Toward an Environmental Sociology of Extractive Economies," Ph.D. dissertation, University of Oregon, 2014.

Chapter 4 The Social Turn

1 For a fascinating analysis at the peak of the social turn from a brilliant historian, see E. J. Hobsbawm, "From Social History to the History of Society," *Daedalus*, 100/1 (1971): 20–45.

2 João José Reis and Everton Sales Souza, "Kátia Mytilineou de Queirós Mattoso," *Afro-Ásia*, 48 (2013): 363–81.

3 Leslie Bethell, *The Abolition of the Brazilian Slave Trade: Britain, Brazil, and the Slave Trade Question, 1807–1869* (Cambridge: Cambridge University Press, 1970); Robert Conrad, *The Destruction of Brazilian Slavery, 1850–1888* (Berkeley: University of California Press, 1972); Robert Brent Toplin, *The Abolition of Slavery in Brazil* (New York: Atheneum, 1972); Stuart B. Schwartz, *Sugar Plantations in the Formation of Brazilian Society, Bahia, 1550–1835* (Cambridge: Cambridge University Press, 1985); A. J. R. Russell-Wood, *The Black Man in Slavery and Freedom in Colonial Brazil* (New York: St. Martin's Press, 1982); João José Reis, *Slave Rebellion in Brazil: The Muslim Uprising of 1835 in Bahia*, trans. Arthur Brakel (Baltimore: Johns Hopkins University Press, 1993).

4 Frederick P. Bowser, *The African Slave in Colonial Peru, 1524–1650* (Stanford, CA: Stanford University Press, 1974); Colin A. Palmer, *Slaves of the White God: Blacks in Colonial Mexico, 1570–1650* (Cambridge, MA: Harvard University Press, 1976).

5 *The Sugarmill: The Socioeconomic Complex of Sugar in Cuba, 1760–1860*, trans. Cedric Belfrage (New York: Monthly Review

Press, 1976). The work was originally published in Spanish in 1964. Moreno Fraginals studied in Mexico in the 1940s with Silvio Zavala.

6 Charles Gibson, *The Aztecs under Spanish Rule: A History of the Indians of the Valley of Mexico, 1519–1810* (Stanford, CA: Stanford University Press, 1964); James Lockhart, *The Nahuas after the Conquest: A Social and Cultural History of the Indians of Central Mexico, Sixteenth through Eighteenth Centuries* (Stanford, CA: Stanford University Press, 1992).

7 John V. Murra, *The Economic Organization of the Inka State* (Greenwich, CT: JAI Press, 1980), originally his doctoral dissertation at the University of Chicago (1955). Nathan Wachtel, *Vision of the Vanquished: The Spanish Conquest of Peru through Indian Eyes (1530–1570)*, trans. Ben Reynolds and Siân Reynolds (New York: Barnes & Noble, 1971), originally pubd as *La Vision des vaincus: les Indiens du Pérou devant la conquête espagnol, 1530–1570* (Paris: Gallimard, 1971); Franklin Pease, *Los últimos Incas del Cuzco* (Lima: P. L. Villanueva, 1972); Luis Valcárcel, *Garcilaso el Inca: visto desde el ángulo indio* (Lima: Imprenta del Museo Nacional, 1939); Steve J. Stern, *Peru's Indian Peoples and the Challenge of the Spanish Conquest: Huamanga to 1640* (Madison: University of Wisconsin Press, 1982); Florencia Mallon, *The Defense of Community in Peru's Central Highlands: Peasant Struggle and Capitalist Transition, 1860–1940* (Princeton, NJ: Princeton University Press, 1983); Karen Spalding, *Huarochirí: A Colonial Province under Inca and Spanish Rule* (Stanford, CA: Stanford University Press, 1984), from her dissertation at the University of California, Berkeley (1967).

8 Eric Van Young, "Rural History," in José Moya, ed., *The Oxford Handbook of Latin American History* (New York: Oxford University Press, 2010), p. 313; François Chevalier, *La Formation des grands domains au Mexique: terre et société aux XVIe–XVIIe siècles* (Paris: Université de Paris, Institut d'Ethnologie, 1952); *Land and Society in Colonial Mexico: The Great Hacienda*, ed. Leslie B. Simpson, trans. Alvin Eustis (Berkeley: University of California Press, 1966).

9 Just a few examples: William B. Taylor, *Landlord and Peasant in Colonial Oaxaca* (Stanford, CA: Stanford University Press, 1972); Marcelo Carmagnani, *Los mecanismos de la vida económica en una sociedad colonial: Chile, 1680–1880* (Santiago: Centro de Investigaciones Diego Barros Arana, 1973); Eric Van Young, *Hacienda and Market in Eighteenth-Century Mexico: The Rural Economy of the Guadalajara Region, 1675–1820* (Berkeley: University of California Press,

1981); Carlos Sempat Assadourian, *El sistema de la economía colonial: mercado interno, regions y espacio económico* (Lima: Instituto de Estudios Peruanos, 1982); Juan Carlos Garavaglia and Jorge D. Gelman, "Rural History of the Río de la Plata," in Raúl Fradkin, ed., *La historia agraria del Río de la Plata colonial: los establecimientos productivos*, 2 vols (Buenos Aires: Centro Editorial de América Latina, 1993), Vol. 1, pp. 7–44.

10 Eric R. Wolf, *Peasant Wars of the Twentieth Century* (New York: Harper & Row, 1969), *Europe and the People without History* (Berkeley: University of California Press, 1982), and *Peasants* (Englewood Cliffs, NJ: Prentice-Hall, 1966); Rodolfo Stavenhagen, *Agrarian Problems and Peasant Movements in Latin America* (Garden City, NY: Doubleday, 1970).

11 John Womack, Jr., *Zapata and the Mexican Revolution* (New York: Random House, 1968), p. ix; Stuart B. Schwartz, *Slaves, Peasants, and Rebels: Reconsidering Brazilian Slavery* (Urbana: University of Illinois Press, 1992); Ciro F. S. Cardoso, *Escravo ou camponês: o protocampesinato negro nas Américas* (São Paulo: Brasiliense, 1987).

12 Kris Lane, *Potosí: The Silver City that Changed the World* (Berkeley: University of California Press, 2019); Peter Bakewell, *Silver and Entrepreneurship in Seventeenth-Century Potosí: The Life and Times of Antonio López de Quiroga* (Albuquerque: University of New Mexico Press, 1988).

13 Robert C. West, *The Mining Community in Northern New Spain: The Parral Mining District* (Berkeley: University of California Press, 1949); Enrique Tandeter, *Coercion and Market: Silver Mining in Colonial Potosí, 1692–1826* (Albuquerque: University of New Mexico Press, 1993), originally pubd as *Coacción y mercado: la minería de la plata en el Potosí colonial, 1692–1826* (Cusco: Centro de Estudios Regionales Andinos, "Bartolomé de las Casas", 1992).

14 Laura de Mello e Souza, *Desclassificados do ouro: a pobreza mineira no século XVIII* (Rio de Janeiro: Graal, 1983). Trained by the great Brazilian historian Fernando Novais, Mello e Souza taught for many years at USP and is currently the chair in Brazilian history at the University of Paris, Sorbonne.

15 John Kicza, *Colonial Entrepreneurs, Families and Business in Bourbon Mexico City* (Albuquerque: University of New Mexico Press, 1983); A. J. R. Russell-Wood, *Fidalgos and Philanthropists: The Santa Casa da Misericórdia of Bahia, 1550–1755* (Berkeley: University of California Press, 1968); Susan M. Socolow, *The Merchants of Buenos Aires, 1778–1810: Family and Commerce* (Cambridge: Cambridge University Press,

1978); Ralph Lee Woodward, Jr., *Class Privilege and Economic Development: The Consulado de Comercio of Guatemala, 1793–1871* (Chapel Hill: University of North Carolina Press, 1966).

16 John Lynch, *The Spanish American Revolutions, 1808–1826* (2nd rev. edn, New York: W. W. Norton, 1986); Jay Kinsbruner, *Independence in Spanish America: Civil Wars, Revolution, and Underdevelopment* (Albuquerque: University of New Mexico Press, 1994); Jaime Rodríguez O., *The Independence of Spanish America* (Cambridge: Cambridge University Press, 1998).

17 D. C. M. Platt, *Business Imperialism, 1840–1930: An Inquiry Based on British Experience in Latin America* (Oxford: Clarendon Press, 1977); Marshall C. Eakin, *British Enterprise in Brazil: The St. John d'el Rey Mining Company and the Morro Velho Gold Mine, 1830–1960* (Durham, NC: Duke University Press, 1989); Carlos Dávila and Rory Miller, eds, *Business History in Latin America: The Experience of Seven Countries*, trans. Garry Mills and Rory Miller (Liverpool: Liverpool University Press, 1999).

18 Francisco C. Weffort, *O populismo na política brasileira* (Rio de Janeiro: Paz e Terra, 1978); Michael Conniff, *Urban Politics in Brazil: The Rise of Populism, 1925–1945* (Pittsburgh: University of Pittsburgh Press, 1981); Gino Germani, *Authoritarianism, Fascism, and National Populism* (New Brunswick, NJ: Transaction Books, 1978).

19 Pablo González Casanova, *Historia del movimiento obrero en América Latina* (Mexico City: Siglo Veintiuno, 1984–5); Angela de Castro Gomes, *A invenção do trabalhismo* (Rio de Janeiro: IUEPRJ; São Paulo: Vértice, 1988).

20 Emilia Viotti da Costa, "Experience versus Structures: New Tendencies in the History of Labor and the Working Class in Latin America – What Do We Gain? What Do We Lose?" *International Labor and Working-Class History*, 36 (1989): 3–24; Daniel James, *Resistance and Integration: Peronism and the Argentine Working Class, 1946–1976* (Cambridge: Cambridge University Press, 1988); John D. French, *The Brazilian Workers' ABC: Class Conflicts and Alliances in Modern São Paulo* (Chapel Hill: University of North Carolina Press, 1992).

21 James P. Brennan, "Latin American Labor History," in Moya, ed., *The Oxford Handbook of Latin American History*, pp. 343–4.

22 For the early period, see Peter DeShazo, *Urban Workers and Labor Unions in Chile, 1902–1927* (Madison: University of Wisconsin Press, 1983); Boris Fausto, *Trabalho urbano e*

conflito social (São Paulo: DIFEL, 1977); Sebastián Marotta, *El movimiento sindical argentino: su genesis y desarrollo*, 3 vols (Buenos Aires: Lacio, 1960).

23 John French and Daniel James, eds, *The Gendered Worlds of Latin American Women Workers: From Household and Factory to the Union Hall and Ballot Box* (Durham, NC: Duke University Press, 1997).

24 Roger Adelson, "Interview with Asunción Lavrin," *The Historian*, 61/1 (1998): 1–14.

25 Ann M. Pescatello, *Power and Pawn: The Female in Iberian Families, Societies, and Cultures* (Westport, CT: Greenwood Press, 1976); Asunción Lavrin, ed., *Latin American Women: Historical Perspectives* (Westport, CT: Greenwood Press, 1978); Maria Beatriz Nizza da Silva, *Sistema de casamento no Brasil colonial* (São Paulo: Editora da Universidade de São Paulo, 1984); Alexandra Parma Cook and Noble David Cook, *Good Faith and Truthful Ignorance: A Case of Transatlantic Bigamy* (Durham, NC: Duke University Press, 1991); Sandra Lauderdale Graham, *House and Street: The Domestic World of Servants and Masters in Nineteenth-Century Rio de Janeiro* (Austin: University of Texas Press, 1992).

26 Silvia Arrom, *The Women of Mexico City, 1790–1857* (Stanford, CA: Stanford University Press, 1985); Patricia Seed, *To Love, Honor, and Obey in Colonial Mexico: Conflicts over Marriage Choice, 1574–1821* (Stanford, CA: Stanford University Press, 1988); Donna J. Guy, *Sex and Danger in Buenos Aires: Prostitution, Family, and Nation in Argentina* (Lincoln: University of Nebraska Press, 1991); Verena Martínez-Alier, *Marriage, Class, and Colour in Nineteenth-Century Cuba: A Study of Racial Attitudes and Sexual Values in a Slave Society* (Cambridge: Cambridge University Press, 1974); Verena Stolcke, *Coffee Planters, Workers, and Wives: Class Conflict and Gender Relations on São Paulo Coffee Plantations, 1850–1980* (New York: St. Martin's Press, 1988).

27 For an excellent analysis, see Heidi Tinsman, "A Paradigm of Our Own: Joan Scott and Latin American History," *American Historical Review*, 113/5 (2008): 1357–74. See also Susan Socolow, "Women in Colonial Latin American History," and Elizabeth Quay Hutchinson, "Women in Modern Latin American History," *Oxford Bibliographies*, www.oxfordbibliographies.com [subscription required].

28 Margaret Randall, *Sandino's Daughters: Testimonies of Nicaraguan Women in Struggle*, ed. Lynda Yanz (Vancouver: New Star, 1981); Domitila Barrios de Chungara with Moema Viezzer, *Let Me Speak! Testimony of Domitila, a Woman of*

the Bolivian Mines, trans. Victoria Ortiz (New York: Monthly Review Press, 1978).

29 For an excellent historiographical essay on this topic from the perspective of popular religiosity, see Reinaldo L. Román and Pamela Voekel, "Popular Religion in Latin American Historiography," in Moya, ed., *The Oxford Handbook of Latin American History*, pp. 454–87.

30 Nancy M. Farriss, *Crown and Clergy in Colonial Mexico, 1759–1821: The Crisis of Ecclesiastical Privilege* (London: Athlone, 1968); *Maya Society under Colonial Rule: The Collective Enterprise of Survival* (Princeton, NJ: Princeton University Press, 1984); *Tongues of Fire: Language and Evangelization in Colonial Mexico* (New York: Oxford University Press, 2018).

31 Robert Ricard, *The Spiritual Conquest of Mexico: An Essay on the Apostolate and the Evangelizing Methods of the Mendicant Orders in New Spain: 1523–1572*, trans. Lesley Byrd Simpson (Berkeley: University of California Press, 1966 [French edn, 1933]). The quote comes from Román and Voekel, "Popular Religion in Latin American Historiography," p. 459.

32 Serge Gruzinski, *Man-Gods in the Mexican Highlands: Indian Power and Colonial Society, 1520–1800*, trans. Eileen Corrigan (Stanford, CA: Stanford University Press, 1989 [French edn, 1985), and *The Mestizo Mind: The Intellectual Dynamics of Colonization and Globalization*, trans. Deke Dusinberre (New York: Routledge, 2002 [French edn, 1999]); Inga Clendinnen, *Ambivalent Conquests: Maya and Spaniard in the Yucatan, 1517–1570* (Cambridge: Cambridge University Press, 1987); Susan Schroeder, *Chimalpahin and the Kingdoms of Chalco* (Tucson: University of Arizona Press, 1991); Robert Haskett, *Indigenous Rulers: An Ethnohistory of Town Government in Colonial Cuernavaca* (Albuquerque: University of New Mexico Press, 1991).

33 Fine examples of earlier, more traditional approaches are Clarence H. Haring, *The Spanish Empire in America* (New York: Oxford University Press, [1947] 1985); John H. Parry, *The Audiencia of New Galicia in the Sixteenth Century: A Study in Spanish Colonial Government* (Cambridge: Cambridge University Press, 1948); and Arthur S. Aiton, *Antonio de Mendoza, First Viceroy of New Spain* (Durham, NC: Duke University Press, 1927). More recent publications include Nicholas P. Cushner, *Lords of the Land: Sugar, Wine, and Jesuit Estates of Coastal Peru, 1600–1763* (Albany: State University of New York Press, 1980); and John Frederick Schwaller, *Origins of Church Wealth in Mexico: Ecclesiastical Revenues*

and Church Finances, 1523–1600 (Albuquerque: University of New Mexico Press, 1985).
34 Mark Burkholder and D. S. Chandler, *From Impotence to Authority: The Spanish Crown and the American Audiencias, 1687–1808* (Columbia: University of Missouri Press, 1977).
35 Some examples of the more traditional approach are Lewis Hanke, *The Spanish Struggle for Justice in the Conquest of America* (Philadelphia: University of Pennsylvania Press, 1949); Silvio A. Zavala, *Las instituciones jurídicas en la conquista de América* (2nd edn, Mexico City: Editorial Porrúa, 1971); Marcel Bataillon and André Saint-Lu, *Las Casas et la défense des Indiens* (Paris: Julliard, 1971). Revisionist works include William B. Taylor, *Drinking, Homicide, and Rebellion in Colonial Mexican Villages* (Stanford, CA: Stanford University Press, 1979); Brian P. Owensby, *Empire of Law and Indian Justice in Colonial Mexico* (Stanford, CA: Stanford University Press, 2008); Rebecca Horn, *Post-conquest Coyoacan: Nahua–Spanish Relations in Central Mexico, 1519–1650* (Stanford, CA: Stanford University Press, 1997).

Chapter 5 Cultural and Other Turns

1 David Szanton, ed., *The Politics of Knowledge: Area Studies and the Disciplines* (Berkeley: University of California Press, 2004), esp. Paul W. Drake and Lisa Hilbink, "Latin American Studies: Theory and Practice," pp. 34–73; and Sonia Álvarez, Arturo Arias, and Charles Hale, "Re-visioning Latin American Studies," *Cultural Anthropology*, 26/2 (2011): 225–46.
2 See, for example, "AHR Forum: Historiographical 'Turns' in Critical Perspective," *American Historical Review*, 177/3 (2012): 698–813, especially James W. Cook, "The Kids Are All Right: On the 'Turning' of Cultural History," pp. 746–71.
3 Peter Burke, *What Is Cultural History?* (3rd edn, Cambridge: Polity, 2019), p. 78.
4 Ibid., p. 3.
5 Antonio Gramsci, *Selections from the Prison Notebooks* (New York: International, 1971); Stuart Hall, "Gramsci's Relevance for the Study of Race and Ethnicity," *Journal of Communication Studies*, 10/2 (1986): 5–27.
6 Burke, *What Is Cultural History?*, p. 59.
7 Karl Marx, *The Eighteenth Brumaire of Louis Bonaparte* (New York: International, 1963), p. 15.
8 Edward Said, *Orientalism* (New York: Random House, 1978); Gayatri Chakravorty Spivak, "Can the Subaltern Speak?," in

Lawrence Grossburg and Cary Nelson, eds, *Marxism and the Interpretation of Culture* (Urbana: University of Illinois Press, 1988), pp. 271–313.

9   Gilbert M. Joseph and Susan Deans-Smith, eds, "Mexico's New Cultural History: una lucha libre," *Hispanic American Historical Review*, 79/2 (1999).

10 Eric Van Young, "The New Cultural History Comes to Old Mexico," ibid., p. 216.

11 William E. French, "Imagining the New Cultural History of Nineteenth-Century Mexico," ibid., p. 249. Sara Castro Klarén and John Charles Chasteen, eds, *Beyond Imagined Communities: Reading and Writing the Nation in Nineteenth-Century Latin America* (Washington, DC: Woodrow Wilson Center Press/Baltimore: Johns Hopkins University Press, 2003).

12 Florencia E. Mallon, "The Promise and Dilemma of Subaltern Studies: Perspectives from Latin American History," *American Historical Review*, 99/5 (1994): 1491–1515, at p. 1501.

13 Originally published in 1962, the key work in English translation is *The Structural Transformation of the Public Sphere*, trans. Thomas Burger and Frederick Lawrence (Cambridge: Polity, 1989).

14 See, for example, Sarah Chambers, *From Subjects to Citizens: Honor, Gender, and Politics in Arequipa, Peru, 1780–1854* (University Park: Pennsylvania State University Press, 1999); Fernando Escalante Gonzalbo, *Ciudadanos imaginarios: memorial de los afanes y desventuras de la virtud y apología del vicio triunfante en la República mexicana: tratado de moral pública* (Mexico City: Colegio de México, 1992); Francisco Gutiérrez Sanín, *Curso y discurso del movimiento plebeyo, 1849–54* (Bogotá: Instituto de Estudios Políticos y Relaciones Internacionales, 1995); Carmen McEvoy, *La utopía republicana: ideales y realidades en la formación de la cultura política peruana, 1871–1919* (Lima: Pontificia Universidad Católica del Perú, 1999).

15 Pablo Piccato, "Public Sphere in Latin America: A Map of the Historiography," *Social History*, 35/2 (2010): 165–92.

16 Ibid., p. 168.

17 See, for example, Elías José Palti, "Recent Studies on the Emergence of a Public Sphere in Latin America," *Latin American Research Review*, 36/2 (2001): 255–87.

18 See, for example, Celso Thomas Castilho, *Slave Emancipation and Transformations in Brazilian Political Citizenship* (Pittsburgh: University of Pittsburgh Press, 2016).

19 Clifford Geertz, *The Interpretation of Cultures: Selected Essays* (New York: Basic Books, 1973); Néstor García Canclini,

Hybrid Cultures: Strategies for Entering and Leaving Modernity (Minneapolis: University of Minnesota Press, 1995 [originally pubd in Spanish in 1990]). For examples of popular culture as everyday culture of the people, see William H. Beezley, *Judas at the Jockey Club* (Lincoln: University of Nebraska Press, 1987), and William H. Beezley, Cheryl English Martin, and William E. French, eds, *Rituals of Rule, Rituals of Resistance: Public Celebrations and Popular Culture in Mexico* (Wilmington, DE: SR Books, 1994).

20 For a discussion of some of the differences between U.S. and Latin American scholars, see Jane S. Jaquette, "Introduction: From Transition to Participation – Women's Movements and Democratic Politics," in Jaquette, ed., *The Women's Movement in Latin America: Feminism and the Transition to Democracy* (Boston: Unwin Hyman, 1989).

21 See Joan Scott, "Gender: A Useful Category of Historical Analysis," *American Historical Review*, 91/5 (1986): 1053–75, and *Gender and the Politics of History* (New York: Columbia University Press, 1988). Scott's pathbreaking essay is the most accessed article ever from the electronic archive of the *American Historical Review*.

22 See Sueann Caulfield, "The History of Gender in the History of Latin America," *Hispanic American Historical Review*, 81/3–4 (2001): 449–90. This excellent essay is part of a special double issue of the *HAHR* on gender history.

23 Some key edited works that demonstrate the development of the research are Marysa Navarro and Virginia Sánchez Korrol, eds, *Women in Latin America and the Caribbean: Restoring Women to History* (Bloomington: Indiana University Press, 1999); Elizabeth Dore and Maxine Molyneux, eds, *Hidden Histories of Gender and the State in Latin America* (Durham, NC: Duke University Press, 2000); William E. French and Katherine Elaine Bliss, eds, *Gender, Sexuality, and Power in Latin America since Independence* (Lanham, MD: Rowman & Littlefield, 2007).

24 For an excellent discussion of this point, see Thomas Miller Klubock, "Writing the History of Women and Gender," *Hispanic American Historical Review*, 81/3–4 (2001): 493–518; the quotation is at p. 518.

25 Martha de Abreu Esteves, *Meninas perdidas: os populares e o cotidiano do amor no Rio de Janeiro da "Belle Epoque"* (Rio de Janeiro: Paz e Terra, 1989); Donna Guy, *Sex and Danger in Buenos Aires: Prostitution, Family, and Nation in Argentina* (Lincoln: University of Nebraska Press, 1991); Sueann Caulfield and Martha de Abreu Esteves, "Fifty Years of Virginity in Rio

de Janeiro: Sexual Politics and Gender Roles in Juridical and Popular Discourse, 1890–1940," *Luso-Brazilian Review*, 30/1 (1993): 47–74.

26 Mary Del Priore, *Ao sul do corpo: condição feminina, maternidades e mentalidades no Brasil Colônia* (Rio de Janeiro: Olympio, 1993); Laura de Mello e Souza, ed., *História da vida privada no Brasil*, Vol. 1: *Cotidiano e vida privada na América Portuguesa* (São Paulo: Companhia das Letras, 1997).

27 Nara Milanich, "The Historiography of Latin American Families," in José Moya, ed., *The Oxford Handbook of Latin American History* (New York: Oxford University Press, 2010), pp. 382–406.

28 Sueann Caulfield, Sarah Chambers, and Lara Putnam, eds, *Honor, Status, and Law in Modern Latin American History* (Durham, NC: Duke University Press, 2005); Lyman L. Johnson and Sonya Lipsett-Rivera, eds, *The Faces of Honor: Sex, Shame, and Violence in Colonial Latin America* (Albuquerque: University of New Mexico Press, 1998).

29 Pete Sigal, ed., *Infamous Desire: Male Homosexuality in Colonial Latin America* (Chicago: University of Chicago Press, 2003).

30 See Matthew Restall, "The New Conquest History," *History Compass*, 10 (2012): 151–60.

Chapter 6 Beyond Latin American History

1 Patricia Nelson Limerick, Clyde Milner II, and Charles E. Rankin, eds, *Trails: Toward a New Western History* (Lawrence: University Press of Kansas, 1991).

2 For two excellent historiographical reviews, see Pekka Hämäläinen and Samuel Truett, "On Borderlands," *Journal of American History*, 98/2 (2011): 338–61; Jeremy Adelman and Stephen Aron, "From Borderlands to Borders: Empires, Nation-States, and the Peoples in Between in North American History," *American Historical Review*, 104/3 (1999): 814–41.

3 Winfried Fluck, Donald Pease, and John Carlos Rowe, *Re-framing the Transnational Turn in American Studies* (Hanover, NH: Dartmouth College Press, 2011); Brian Edwards and Dilip Parameshwar Gaonkar, eds, *Globalizing American Studies* (Chicago: University of Chicago Press, 2010); Kristin Hoganson and Jay Sexton, eds, *Crossing Empires: Taking U.S. History into Transimperial Terrain* (Durham, NC: Duke University Press, 2020).

4 See Micol Seigel, "Beyond Compare: Comparative Method

after the Transnational Turn," *Radical History Review*, 91 (Winter 2005): 62–90.
5 James E. Sanders, *The Vanguard of the Atlantic World: Creating Modernity, Nation, and Democracy in Nineteenth-Century Latin America* (Durham, NC: Duke University Press, 2014); Jorge Cañizares-Esguerra, *How to Write the History of the New World: Histories, Epistemologies and Identities in the Eighteenth-Century Atlantic World* (Stanford, CA: Stanford University Press, 2001); Pablo F. Gómez, *The Experiential Caribbean: Creating Knowledge and Healing in the Early Modern Atlantic* (Chapel Hill: University of North Carolina Press, 2017).
6 See, for example, Adam McKeown, *Chinese Migrant Networks and Cultural Change: Peru, Chicago, and Hawaii, 1900–1936* (Chicago: University of Chicago Press, 2001); Jose C. Moya and Adam McKeown, *World Migration in the Long Twentieth Century* (Washington, DC: American Historical Association, 2011).
7 Ida Altman and James Horn, eds, *"To Make America": European Emigration in the Early Modern Period* (Berkeley: University of California Press, 1991); Theresa Alfaro Velkamp, *So Far from Allah, So Close to Mexico: Middle Eastern Immigrants in Modern Mexico* (Austin: University of Texas Press, 2007); Jeffrey Lesser, *A Discontented Diaspora: Japanese Brazilians and the Meanings of Ethnic Militancy, 1960–1980* (Durham, NC: Duke University Press, 2007); Kathleen López, *Chinese Cubans: A Transnational History* (Chapel Hill: University of North Carolina Press, 2013); Rosemarijn Hoefte, *In Place of Slavery: A Social History of British Indian and Javanese Laborers in Suriname* (Gainesville: University Press of Florida, 1998).
8 Gilbert M. Joseph, Catherine C. LeGrand, and Ricardo D. Salvatore, eds, *Close Encounters of Empire: Writing the Culture History of U.S.–Latin American Relations* (Durham, NC: Duke University Press, 1998), pp. 3–4.
9 Sandhya Shukla and Heidi Tinsman, eds, *Imagining Our Americas: Toward a Transnational Frame* (Durham, NC: Duke University Press, 2007), p. 6.
10 José Amador, *Medicine and Nation Building in the Americas, 1890–1940* (Nashville: Vanderbilt University Press, 2015); Marcos Cueto, *Missionaries of Science: The Rockefeller Foundation and Latin America* (Bloomington: Indiana University Press, 1994); Diego Armus, ed., *Disease in the History of Modern Latin America: From Malaria to AIDS* (Durham, NC: Duke University Press, 2003).

11 See, for example, Stephen Haber, ed., *How Latin America Fell Behind: Essays on the Economic Histories of Brazil and Mexico* (Stanford, CA: Stanford University Press, 1997), and *Political Institutions and Economic Growth in Latin America: Essays in Policy, History, and Political Economy* (Stanford, CA: Hoover Institution Press, 2000); Gail D. Triner, *Banking and Economic Development: Brazil, 1889–1930* (New York: Palgrave Macmillan, 2000); Anne G. Hanley, *Native Capital: Financial Institutions and Economic Development in São Paulo, 1850–1920* (Stanford, CA: Stanford University Press, 2005).

12 Alison Games, "Atlantic History: Definitions, Challenges, and Opportunities," *American Historical Review*, 111/3 (2006): 741–57; the quote is from p. 745.

13 Ibid., and Jorge Cañizares-Esguerra and Benjamin Breen, "Hybrid Atlantics: Future Directions for the History of the Atlantic World," *History Compass*, 11/8 (2013): 597–609.

14 Ira Berlin, *Many Thousands Gone: The First Two Centuries of Slavery in North America* (Cambridge, MA: Belknap Press, 1998); Jane Landers, *Atlantic Creoles in the Age of Revolutions* (Cambridge, MA: Harvard University Press, 2010); Robin Cohen and Paola Toninato, eds, *The Creolization Reader: Studies in Mixed Identities and Cultures* (New York: Routledge, 2009).

15 Sidney W. Mintz, *Sweetness and Power: The Place of Sugar in Modern History* (New York: Viking, 1985); Judith Carney, *Black Rice: The African Origins of Rice Cultivation in the Americas* (Cambridge, MA: Harvard University Press, 2001); Marcy Norton, *Sacred Gifts, Profane Pleasures: A History of Tobacco and Chocolate in the Atlantic World* (Ithaca, NY: Cornell University Press, 2008); Molly A. Warsh, *American Baroque: Pearls and the Nature of Empire, 1492–1700* (Chapel Hill: University of North Carolina Press, 2018); Kris Lane, *Color of Paradise: The Emerald in the Age of Gunpowder Empires* (New Haven, CT: Yale University Press, 2010).

16 John Thornton, *Africa and Africans in the Making of the Atlantic World, 1400–1800* (2nd edn, New York: Cambridge University Press, 1998); Linda M. Heywood, ed., *Central Africans and Cultural Transformations in the American Diaspora* (New York: Cambridge University Press, 2002); Joseph C. Miller, *Way of Death: Merchant Capitalism and the Angolan Slave Trade, 1730–1830* (Madison: University of Wisconsin Press, 1988); Walter Hawthorne, *From Africa to Brazil: Culture, Identity, and an Atlantic Slave Trade, 1600–1830* (New York: Cambridge University Press, 2010);

David Wheat, *Atlantic Africa and the Spanish Caribbean, 1570–1640* (Chapel Hill: University of North Carolina Press, 2016); and Mariana Candido, *An African Slaving Port and the Atlantic World: Benguela and Its Hinterland* (Cambridge: Cambridge University Press, 2013).

17 Some outstanding examples of social scientists contributing to our historical understanding of race in Latin America (to cite just a few) are Marvin Harris, *Patterns of Race in the Americas* (New York: W. W. Norton, 1964); Peter Wade, *Race and Ethnicity in Latin America* (London: Pluto Press, 1997); Kwame Dixon and John Burdick, eds, *Comparative Perspectives on Afro-Latin America* (Gainesville: University Press of Florida, 2012); Edward E. Telles, ed., *Pigmentocracies: Ethnicity, Race, and Color in Latin America* (Chapel Hill: University of North Carolina Press, 2014); Tianna S. Paschel, *Becoming Black Political Subjects: Movements and Ethno-Racial Rights in Colombia and Brazil* (Princeton, NJ: Princeton University Press, 2016).

18 For one of the most influential texts, see Michael Omni and Howard Winant, *Racial Formation in the United States* (New York: Routledge, 1986).

19 Marisol de la Cadena, *Indigenous Mestizos: The Politics of Race and Culture in Cuzco, 1919–1991* (Durham, NC: Duke University Press, 2000); Greg Grandin, *The Blood of Guatemala: A History of Race and Nation* (Durham, NC: Duke University Press, 2000); Brooke Larson, *Trials of Nation Making: Liberalism, Race, and Ethnicity in the Andes* (Cambridge: Cambridge University Press, 2004).

20 For just a few examples of works that examine race and national narratives, see Alejandro de la Fuente, *A Nation for All: Race, Inequality and Politics in Twentieth-Century Cuba* (Chapel Hill: University of North Carolina Press, 2001); Michael E. Stanfield, *Of Beasts and Beauty: Gender, Race, and Identity in Colombia* (Austin: University of Texas Press, 2013); Winthrop R. Wright, *Café con leche: Race, Class, and National Image in Venezuela* (Austin: University of Texas Press, 1990); Barbara Weinstein, *The Color of Modernity: São Paulo and the Making of Race and Nations in Brazil* (Durham, NC: Duke University Press, 2015); Thomas E. Skidmore, *Black into White: Race and Nationality in Brazilian Thought* (Durham, NC: Duke University Press, 1993).

21 Robert J. Cottrol, *The Long Lingering Shadow: Slavery, Race, and Law in the American Hemisphere* (Athens: University of Georgia Press, 2013); Mara Loveman, *National Colors: Racial Classification and the State in Latin America* (Oxford:

Oxford University Press, 2014); Melissa Nobles, *Shades of Citizenship: Race and the Census in Modern Politics* (Stanford, CA: Stanford University Press, 2000); Marcos Chor Maio and Ricardo Ventura Santos, eds, *Raça, ciência e sociedade* (Rio de Janeiro: Editôra Fiocruz, 1996); Alejandro de la Fuente and Ariela J. Gross, *Becoming Free, Becoming Black: Race, Freedom, and Law in Cuba, Virginia, and Louisiana* (New York: Cambridge University Press, 2020).

22 See "Introduction: Finding the 'Latin American' in Latin American Environmental History," in John Soluri, Claudia Leal, and José Augusto Pádua, eds, *A Living Past: Environmental Histories of Modern Latin America* (New York: Berghahn Books, 2018); Mark Carey, "Latin American Environmental History: Current Trends, Interdisciplinary Insights, and Future Directions," *Environmental History*, 14/2 (2009): 221–52; and Germán Palacio, "An Eco-Political Vision for an Environmental History: Toward a Latin American and North American Research Partnership," *Environmental History*, 17/4 (2012): 725–43.

23 Arij Ouweneel, *Shadows over Anáhuac: An Ecological Interpretation of Crisis and Development in Central Mexico, 1730–1800* (Albuquerque: University of New Mexico Press, 1996); William W. Dunmire, *Gardens of New Spain: How Mediterranean Plants and Foods Changed America* (Austin: University of Texas Press, 2004); Judith A. Carney and Richard Nicholas Rosomoff, *In the Shadow of Slavery: Africa's Botanical Legacy in the Atlantic World* (Berkeley: University of California Press, 2009).

24 Nicholas A. Robins, *Mercury, Mining, and Empire: The Human and Ecological Cost of Colonial Silver Mining in the Andes* (Bloomington: Indiana University Press, 2011); Inés Herrera Canales and Eloy González Marín, *Mining, Metallurgy, and the Environment in Mexico during the Twentieth Century* (Ottawa: International Council on Metals and the Environment, 1995).

25 John Soluri, *Banana Cultures: Agriculture, Consumption, and Environmental Change in Honduras and the United States* (Austin: University of Texas Press, 2005); Sterling Evans, *Bound in Twine: The History and Ecology of the Henequen–Wheat Complex for Mexico and the American and Canadian Plains, 1880–1950* (College Station: Texas A&M University Press, 2007); Thomas D. Rogers, *The Deepest Wounds: A Labor and Environmental History of Sugar in Northeast Brazil* (Chapel Hill: University of North Carolina Press, 2010); Reinaldo Funes Monzote, *From Rainforest to Cane Field in Cuba: An Environmental History Since 1492*, trans. Alex

Martin (Chapel Hill: University of North Carolina Press, 2008); Arturo Warman, *Corn and Capitalism: How a Botanical Bastard Grew to Global Dominance*, trans. Nancy L. Westrate (Chapel Hill: University of North Carolina Press, 2003).

26 Lane Simonian, *Defending the Land of the Jaguar: A History of Conservation in Mexico* (Austin: University of Texas Press, 1995); Emily Wakild, *Revolutionary Parks: Conservation, Social Justice, and Mexico's National Parks, 1910–1940* (Tucson: University of Arizona Press, 2011).

27 Patricia Romero Lankao, *Obra hidráulica en la ciudad de México y su impacto socioambiental, 1880–1990* (Mexico City: Instituto Mora, 1999); Sonya Lipsett-Rivera, *To Defend Our Water with the Blood of Our Veins: The Struggle for Resources in Colonial Puebla* (Albuquerque: University of New Mexico Press, 1999); Mikael Wolf, *Watering the Revolution: An Environmental and Technological History of Agrarian Reform in Mexico* (Durham, NC: Duke University Press, 2017).

28 Stuart B. Schwartz, *Sea of Storms: A History of Hurricanes in the Caribbean from Columbus to Katrina* (Princeton, NJ: Princeton University Press, 2015); Mark Carey, *In the Shadow of Melting Glaciers: Climate Change and Andean Society* (Oxford: Oxford University Press, 2010); César N. Caviedes, *El Niño in History: Storming through the Ages* (Gainesville: University Press of Florida, 2001).

29 See, for example, Fernando Ortiz Monasterio, *Tierra profanada: historia ambiental de México* (Mexico City: Instituto Nacional de Antropología e Historia, 1987); Germán Palacio, *Fiebre de la tierra caliente: una historia ambiental de Colombia, 1850–1930* (Bogotá: ILSA-UNAL-Leticia, 2005); Shawn William Miller, *An Environmental History of Latin America* (Cambridge: Cambridge University Press, 2007); John Soluri, Claudia Leal, and José Augusto Pádua, eds, *A Living Past: Environmental Histories of Modern Latin America* (New York: Berghahn Books, 2018).

30 Martha Few and Zeb Tortorici, eds, *Centering Animals in Latin American History* (Durham, NC: Duke University Press, 2013).

31 See the special issue of *the Hispanic American Historical Review* on "Science and Medicine in Latin America," 91/3 (2011), especially Simone Petraglia Kropf and Gilberto Hochman, "From the Beginnings: Debates on the History of Science in Brazil," pp. 391–408; Stuart McCook, "Focus: Global Currents in National Histories of Science: The 'Global Turn' and the History of Science in Latin America," *Isis*, 104/4 (2013): 773–6; the introduction to Eden Medina, Ivan da Costa

Marques, and Christina Holmes, eds, *Beyond Imported Magic: Essays on Science, Technology, and Society in Latin America* (Cambridge, MA: MIT Press, 2014); and Pablo Kraimer and Hebe Vessuri, "Latin American Science, Technology, and Society: A Historical and Reflexive Approach," *Tapuya: Latin American Science, Technology and Society*, 1/1 (2018): 17–37.

32 Nancy Stepan, *Beginnings of Brazilian Science: Oswaldo Cruz, Medical Research and Policy, 1890–1920* (New York: Science History Publications, 1976); Simon Schwartzman, *A Space for Science: The Development of the Scientific Community in Brazil* (University Park: Pennsylvania State University Press, 1991 [1st edn in Portuguese, 1979]).

33 Ángel Guirao Vierna, *La Real Expedición Botánica a Nueva España* (Madrid: CSIC, 1987); Daniela Bleichmar, *Visible Empire: Botanical Expeditions and Visual Culture in the Hispanic Enlightenment* (Chicago: University of Chicago Press, 2012); Daniela Bleichmar, Paula De Vos, Kristin Huffine, and Kevin Sheehan, *Science in the Spanish and Portuguese Empires, 1500–1800* (Stanford, CA: Stanford University Press, 2009).

34 Stuart B. Schwartz, *All Can Be Saved: Religious Tolerance and Salvation in the Iberian Atlantic World* (New Haven, CT: Yale University Press, 2008); Jorge Cañizares-Esguerra, *How to Write the History of the New World: Histories, Epistemologies and Identities in the Eighteenth-Century Atlantic World* (Stanford, CA: Stanford University Press, 2001), and *Nature, Empire, and Nation: Explorations of the History of Science in the Iberian World* (Stanford, CA: Stanford University Press, 2006); Antonio Barrera-Osorio, *Experiencing Nature: The Spanish American Empire and the Early Scientific Revolution* (Austin: University of Texas Press, 2006).

35 Hugh Cagle, *Assembling the Tropics: Science and Medicine in Portugal's Empire, 1450–1700* (New York: Cambridge University Press, 2019); Pablo F. Gómez, *The Experiential Caribbean: Creating Knowledge and Healing in the Early Modern Atlantic* (Chapel Hill: University of North Carolina Press, 2017); Julyan Peard, *Race, Place, and Medicine: The Idea of the Tropics in Nineteenth-Century Brazilian Medicine* (Durham, NC: Duke University Press, 2000); Steven Palmer, *From Popular Medicine to Medical Populism: Doctors, Healers, and Public Power in Costa Rica, 1800–1940* (Durham, NC: Duke University Press, 2003); James H. Sweet, *Domingos Álvares, African Healing, and the Intellectual History of the Atlantic World* (Chapel Hill: University of North Carolina Press, 2013).

36 Regina Horta Duarte, "Between the National and the Universal:

Natural History Networks in Latin America in the Nineteenth and Twentieth Centuries," *Isis*, 104/4 (2013): 777–87, at p. 783.
37 Kropf and Hochman, "From the Beginnings: Debates on the History of Science in Brazil," p. 397.
38 Marcos Cueto, *Excelencia científica en la periferia: actividades científicas e investigación biomédica en el Perú, 1890–1950* (Lima: Tarea, 1989); Anne-Emanuelle Birn, *Marriage of Convenience: Rockefeller International Health and Revolutionary Mexico* (Rochester, NY: University of Rochester Press, 2006); Stuart McCook, *States of Nature: Science, Agriculture, and Environment in the Spanish Caribbean, 1760–1940* (Austin: University of Texas Press, 2002).
39 Noble David Cook, *Born to Die: Disease and New World Conquest, 1492–1650* (Cambridge: Cambridge University Press, 1998); Diego Armus, *Disease in the History of Modern Latin America: From Malaria to AIDS* (Durham, NC: Duke University Press, 2003); Suzanne Austin Alchon, *A Pest in the Land: New World Epidemics in a Global Perspective* (Albuquerque: University of New Mexico Press, 2003); Marcos Cueto, *Cold War, Deadly Fevers: Malaria Eradication in Mexico, 1955–1975* (Baltimore: Johns Hopkins University Press, 2007); Shawn Smallman, *The AIDS Pandemic in Latin America* (Chapel Hill: University of North Carolina Press, 2007).
40 Jaime Larry Benchimol, *Manguinhos do sonho a vida: a ciência na Belle Epoque* (Rio de Janeiro: Fiocruz, 1990); Gilberto Hochman, *A era do saneamento: as bases da política de saúde pública no Brasil* (São Paulo: Editora Hucitec, 1998); Emilio Quevedo and Carlos Agudelo, *Café y gusanos, mosquitos y petróleo: el tránsito desde la higiene hacia la medicina tropical y la salud pública en Colombia, 1873–1953* (Bogotá: Universidad Nacional, 2004); Ann Zulawski, *Unequal Cures: Public Health and Political Change in Bolivia, 1900–1950* (Durham, NC: Duke University Press, 2007).
41 Anne-Emanuelle Birn and Raúl Necochea López, "Footprints on the Future: Looking Forward to the History of Health and Medicine in Latin America in the Twenty-First Century," *Hispanic American Historical Review*, 91/3 (2011): 503–27; Laura Briggs, *Reproducing Empire: Race, Sex, Science, and U.S. Imperialism in Puerto Rico* (Berkeley: University of California Press, 2002); Julia Rodríguez, *Civilizing Argentina: Science, Medicine, and the Modern State* (Chapel Hill: University of North Carolina Press, 2006); P. Sean Brotherton, *Revolutionary*

Medicine: Health and the Body in Post-Soviet Cuba (Durham, NC: Duke University Press, 2012).

42 Maria Freire, *Mulheres, mães e médicos: discurso maternalista no Brasil* (Rio de Janeiro: Editorial FGV, 2009); Nara Milanich, *Children of Fate: Childhood, Class, and the State in Chile, 1850–1930* (Durham, NC: Duke University Press, 2009); Katherine Elaine Bliss, *Compromised Positions: Prostitution, Public Health, and Gender Politics in Revolutionary Mexico City* (University Park: Pennsylvania State University Press, 2001); Donna Guy, *White Slavery and Mothers Alive and Dead: The Troubled Meeting of Sex, Gender, Public Health, and Progress in Latin America* (Lincoln: University of Nebraska Press, 2000); Alfredo López Austin, *Cuerpo humano e ideología: las concepciones de los antiguos Nahuas* (Mexico City: Universidad Nacional Autónoma de México, 1980).

43 Juan José Saldaña, ed., *Historia social de las ciencias en América Latina* (Mexico City: Coordinación de Humanidades, 1996); Mário Guimarães Ferri and Shozo Motoyama, eds, *História das ciências no Brasil* (São Paulo: EPU/EDUSP, 1979).

44 Kraimer and Vessuri, "Latin American Science, Technology, and Society"; Eden Medina, Ivan da Costa Marques, and Christina Holmes, eds, *Beyond Imported Magic: Essays on Science, Technology, and Society in Latin America* (Cambridge, MA: MIT Press, 2014); Araceli Tinajero and J. Brian Freeman, eds, *Technology and Culture in Twentieth-Century Mexico* (Tuscaloosa: University of Alabama Press, 2013).

Epilogue: The Future of Latin American History

1 Walter D. Mignolo, *The Idea of Latin America* (Malden, MA: Blackwell, 2005), p. 233.
2 Mauricio Tenorio-Trillo, *Latin America: The Allure and Power of an Idea* (Chicago: University of Chicago Press, 2017), p. 164.

Further Reading

Rather than creating a list from the vast and rich literature on the history of Latin America, I have gathered in this section the most valuable historiographical essays in helping me construct this book. The Oxford Bibliographies, at www.oxfordbibliographies.com, have been especially useful, and many of them are packed with helpful insights into the many subfields of Latin American history.

Chapter 1 What Is Latin America?

Mark T. Berger, *Under Northern Eyes: Latin American Studies and U.S. Hegemony in the Americas, 1898–1990* (Bloomington: Indiana University Press, 1995).

Leslie Bethell, ed., *The Cambridge History of Latin America*, 11 vols (Cambridge: Cambridge University Press, 1984–2009).

Paul W. Drake and Lisa Hilbink, "Latin American Studies: Theory and Practice," in David Szanton, ed., *The Politics of Knowledge: Area Studies and the Disciplines* (Berkeley: University of California Press, 2004), pp. 34–73.

Thomas H. Holloway, ed., *A Companion to Latin American History* (Malden, MA: Wiley-Blackwell, 2011).

José Moya, ed., *The Oxford Handbook of Latin American History* (New York: Oxford University Press, 2010).

Chapter 2 The Pioneering Generations

Howard F. Cline, comp. and ed., *Latin American History: Essays on Its Study and Teaching, 1898–1965*, 2 vols (Austin: University of Texas Press, 1967).

Helen Delpar, *Looking South: The Evolution of Latin Americanist Scholarship in the United States, 1850–1975* (Tuscaloosa: University of Alabama Press, 2008).

Ricardo Donato Salvatore, *Disciplinary Conquest: U.S. Scholars in South America, 1900–1945* (Durham, NC: Duke University Press, 2016).

Guillermo Zermeño Padilla, "Mexican Historical Writing," in Axel Schneider and Daniel Woolf, eds, *The Oxford History of Historical Writing*, Vol. 5: *Historical Writing since 1945* (New York: Oxford University Press, 2011), pp. 454–72.

Chapter 3 The Economic and Quantitative Turns

Victor Bulmer-Thomas, John H. Coatsworth, and Roberto Cortés Conde, eds., *The Cambridge Economic History of Latin America*, 2 vols (Cambridge: Cambridge University Press, 2006).

John H. Coatsworth and William R. Summerhill, "The New Economic History of Latin America: Evolution and Recent Contributions," in José Moya, ed., *The Oxford Handbook of Latin American History* (New York: Oxford University Press, 2010), pp. 407–23.

Stanley J. Stein and Roberto Cortés Conde, eds, *Latin America: A Guide to Economic History, 1830–1930* (Berkeley: University of California Press, 1977).

Chapter 4 The Social Turn

E. J. Hobsbawm, "From Social History to the History of Society," *Daedalus*, 100/1 (1971): 20–45.

Jane S. Jaquette, "Introduction: From Transition to Participation – Women's Movements and Democratic Politics," in Jaquette, ed., *The Women's Movement in*

Latin America: Feminism and the Transition to Democracy (Boston: Unwin Hyman, 1989).

Susan Socolow, "Women in Colonial Latin American History," and Elizabeth Quay Hutchinson, "Women in Modern Latin American History," *Oxford Bibliographies*, www.oxfordbibliographies.com.

Chapter 5 Cultural and Other Turns

"AHR Forum: Historiographical 'Turns' in Critical Perspective," *American Historical Review*, 177/3 (2012): 698–813.

Peter Burke, *What Is Cultural History?* (3rd edn, Cambridge: Polity, 2019).

Sueann Caulfield, "The History of Gender in the History of Latin America," *Hispanic American Historical Review*, 81/3–4 (2001): 449–90.

Gilbert M. Joseph, Catherine C. LeGrand, and Ricardo D. Salvatore, eds, *Close Encounters of Empire: Writing the Cultural History of U.S.–Latin American Relations* (Durham, NC: Duke University Press, 1998).

Thomas Miller Klubock, "Writing the History of Women and Gender," *Hispanic American Historical Review*, 81/3–4 (2001): 493–518.

Florencia E. Mallon, "The Promise and Dilemma of Subaltern Studies: Perspectives from Latin American History," *American Historical Review*, 99/5 (1994): 1491–515.

Elías José Palti, "Recent Studies on the Emergence of a Public Sphere in Latin America," *Latin American Research Review*, 36/2 (2001): 255–87.

Pablo Piccato, "Public Sphere in Latin America: A Map of the Historiography," *Social History*, 35/2 (2010): 165–92.

Matthew Restall, "The New Conquest History," *History Compass*, 10 (2012): 151–60.

Heidi Tinsman, "A Paradigm of Our Own: Joan Scott and Latin American History," *American Historical Review*, 113/5 (2008): 1357–74.

Chapter 6 Beyond Latin American History

Jeremy Adelman and Stephen Aron, "From Borderlands to Borders: Empires, Nation-States, and the Peoples in between in North American History," *American Historical Review*, 104/3 (1999): 814–41.

Anne-Emanuelle Birn and Raúl Necochea López, "Footprints on the Future: Looking Forward to the History of Health and Medicine in Latin America in the Twenty-First Century," *Hispanic American Historical Review*, 91/3 (2011): 503–27.

Jorge Cañizares-Esguerra and Benjamin Breen, "Hybrid Atlantics: Future Directions for the History of the Atlantic World," *History Compass*, 11/8 (2013): 597–609.

Mark Carey, "Latin American Environmental History: Current Trends, Interdisciplinary Insights, and Future Directions," *Environmental History*, 14/2 (2009): 221–52.

"Focus: Global Currents in National Histories of Science: The 'Global Turn' and the History of Science in Latin America," *ISIS*, 104/4 (2013) [special issue].

Alison Games, "Atlantic History: Definitions, Challenges, and Opportunities," *American Historical Review*, 111/3 (2006): 741–57.

Pekka Hämäläinen and Samuel Truett, "On Borderlands," *Journal of American History*, 98/2 (2011): 338–61.

Pablo Kraimer and Hebe Vessuri, "Latin American Science, Technology, and Society: A Historical and Reflexive Approach," *Tapuya: Latin American Science, Technology and Society*, 1/1 (2018): 17–37.

Eden Medina, Ivan da Costa Marques, and Christina Holmes, eds, *Beyond Imported Magic: Essays on Science, Technology, and Society in Latin America* (Cambridge, MA: MIT Press, 2014).

Germán Palacio, "An Eco-Political Vision for an Environmental History: Toward a Latin American and North American Research Partnership," *Environmental History*, 17/4 (2012): 725–43.

"Science and Medicine in Latin America," *Hispanic American Historical Review*, 91/3 (2011) [special issue].

John Soluri, Claudia Leal, and José Augusto Pádua, eds, *A*

Living Past: Environmental Histories of Modern Latin America (New York: Berghahn Books, 2018).

Epilogue: The Future of Latin American History

Sonia Álvarez, Arturo Arias, and Charles Hale, "Re-visioning Latin American Studies," *Cultural Anthropology*, 26/2 (2011): 225–46.
Walter D. Mignolo, *The Idea of Latin America* (Malden, MA: Blackwell, 2005).
Mauricio Tenorio-Trillo, *Latin America: The Allure and Power of an Idea* (Chicago: University of Chicago Press, 2017).

Selected General Histories of Latin America

John Charles Chasteen, *Born in Blood and Fire: A Concise History of Latin America* (4th edn, New York: W. W. Norton, 2016).
Marshall C. Eakin, *The History of Latin America: Collision of Cultures* (New York: Palgrave Macmillan, 2007).
Thomas E. Skidmore, Peter H. Smith, and James N. Green, *Modern Latin America* (8th edn, New York: Oxford University Press, 2014).
Edwin Williamson, *The Penguin History of Latin America* (rev. edn, London: Penguin, 2009).

Index

abolition 51–7
Africa and Africans 16, 107, 108
Afrodescendants 8, 12, 111, 117
agency 4, 53, 56, 59, 62, 67, 68, 79, 85, 88, 106–8, 117–18
Aguirre Beltrán, Gonzalo 58
Alamán, Lucas 22
Alberro, Solange 91
Allende, Salvador 44
Alonso, Ana María 90
Altamira, Rafael 29
American Council of Learned Societies 10
American Historical Association (AHA) 2, 23, 27
American Historical Review 84
American Society of Ethnohistory 58
American studies 100–1
Andean region 59, 60, 61, 92–4
Anderson, Benedict 22, 83
Anglo-Saxon America 8–9
Annales School 28, 30–1, 41–3, 53, 61, 64, 70–1, 78, 91

anthropology 24, 42, 51, 61, 78, 79, 82–3, 89, 90, 92
area studies 10, 36, 76–7, 103, 123
Argentina 17
  historical community 28, 30, 35
Arrom, Silvia, 69
Atlantic world history 4, 78, 85, 97, 106–10, 119, 122
Australia 59
authoritarianism 71–2, 76, 121
Aztecs/Nahuas 19, 23, 29, 34, 57–9

Babini, José 115
Bailyn, Bernard 106
Bakewell, Peter 63
Bancroft, Hubert Howe 21–2, 24, 27
Bandelier, Adolph 21
Barros Arana, Diego 22
Barthes, Roland 80
Beckert, Sven 105
Beezley, William 89
Bergquist, Charles 67
Berlin, Ira 108
Bethell, Leslie 54, 73

Black Legend 24
Blakemore, Harold 31
Bloch, Marc 31
Bolívar, Simón 8
Bolton, Herbert Eugene 26–8, 31, 33, 97–8
Borah, Woodrow 27, 33, 40
borderlands 4, 27, 78, 97–100, 102, 103, 120, 122
Bourbon Reforms 72
Bourdieu, Pierre 79–80, 90, 116
Bourne, Edward Gaylord 23–4
Boxer, Charles 31, 64
Brading, David 63
Braudel, Fernand 42, 60
Brazil 11, 13, 17, 22
  graduate programs in 2, 26
  racial categories 12
  slavery 7
Brennan, James 67
Bricker, Victoria 93
Bulletin of Latin American Research 12, 73
Burgos-Debray, Elisabeth 69
Burke, Peter 78
Burkhart, Louise 93
Burkholder, Mark 72
Burns, E. Bradford 14–15, 49, 73
business history 66

Cambridge History of Latin America 15–16, 73
Canada 2, 123
Candido, Mariana 109–10
Cañizares-Esguerra, Jorge 117
capitalism 46–7, 57, 61, 76
  new history of 105
Cárdenas, Lázaro 66–7
Cardoso, Ciro F. S. 43, 62
Cardoso, Fernando Henrique 48, 105
Caribbean 6, 10, 11, 16, 60, 107

decolonization 14
slavery 7
Carrasco Pizana, Pedro 59
Castro, Fidel 37
Catholicism 22, 24, 32, 116
spiritual conquest/
  evangelization 70–1, 92–3
Central America 72, 76, 91, 103
Césaire, Aimé 81, 111
Chandler, D. S. 72
Chapman, Charles Edward 14, 25, 27
Charles V 19
Chartier, Roger 78
Chasteen, John Charles 15
Chaunu, Huguette 42, 106
Chaunu, Pierre 42, 106
Chevalier, François 60–1, 87
Chile
  historical community in 28
China 123, 126
citizenship 86–8, 93–4
class (social) 91
Clayton, Lawrence 15
Clendinnen, Inga 59, 92
climate 114
Cline, Howard 33, 34
Cold War 3, 9, 36, 49, 102, 121, 122
Colegio de México 29
Colonial Latin American Historical Review 73
colonialism 19, 24, 27, 82, 116, 118
Columbia University 33, 52, 81, 87
Columbian Moment 6, 16
Columbus, Christopher 6, 16, 18, 19, 21, 107
Comisión Económica para América Latina (CEPAL)/
Economic Comission for Latin America 11, 47

Index 157

commodities
  bananas 47, 114
  beef 47
  chocolate 108
  coffee 40, 47, 61, 105, 108
  commodity chains 105, 108
  copper 46, 47
  cotton 40, 105, 108
  diamonds 64–5
  dyes 46, 65
  emeralds 108
  gold 46, 65
  guano 114
  henequen 114
  oil 114
  pearls 108
  rice 108
  rubber 113
  silver 40, 46, 65
  sugar 47, 61, 65, 108, 114
  tin 46, 47
tobacco 108
  wheat 47
Conference on Latin American History (CLAH) 1–2, 25, 110
Conniff, Michael 15
Conrad, Robert 54
Cook, Noble David 40
Cook, Sherburne 33, 40
Cortés, Hernán 19, 21, 68
Cosío Villegas, Daniel 29–30
Costa, Emilia Viotti da 53, 59
creolization 107
criollos/creoles 7, 9, 72
Crosby, Alfred 113, 118
Crow, John A. 14
Cruz, Sor Juana Inés de la 68
Cuba 13, 17, 55, 76
Cuban Revolution 4, 37, 44, 75, 84, 121
Cueto, Marcos 118
cultural studies 51, 78

cultural turn/history 39, 43, 73, 75–95, 111, 116, 123
culture 78–9, 82–3
Cumberland, Charles 33
Cunha, Euclídes da 26
Curtin, Philip 108–9
Cushman, Greg 114

Damas, Léon 111
Dean, Warren 113
debt crisis 49
Degler, Carl 52, 111
DeLay, Brian 99
democratization 76
demographic history 33, 40, 92, 118
demography 6–7, 110
dependency theories 44–50, 104–5, 116
Derrida, Jacques 69, 79–80
Díaz, Porfirio 25
diplomatic history 33
disease 6, 113, 118
Dobyns, Henry 40
Doherty Foundation 37
Dominican Republic 55
drugs and drug trafficking 104
Dunkerley, James 72
Dutch empire 54

Earle, Rebecca 93
economic history 33, 34, 36–50, 104–6
economics 41, 48, 51, 75, 105
elections and electoral politics 85–6
Elliott, J. H. 31
Eltis, David 109
Emory University 109
Engerman, Stanley 41
Enlightenment 81, 86, 117
environmental history 112–15
Ethnogeographic Board 10
ethnohistory 57, 70–1

Europe
  empires in the Americas 7, 10, 97, 99, 107
  historical community in 2–3, 38, 94, 96–7, 123
Europeans 6–10, 18, 97, 99, 113, 117
Evans, Peter 48
Evans, Sterling 114

Facultad Latinoamericana de Ciencias Sociales (FLACSO)/ Latin American Social Sciences Faculty 11–12
Faletto, Enzo 48
Fanon, Frantz 81
Farriss, Nancy 59, 70, 92
Febvre, Lucien 31
First World War 3, 32, 49
Florescano, Enrique 42
Fogel, Robert 41, 105
Fondo de Cultura Económica 30
Ford Foundation 36, 37
Foster, George 58
Foucault, Michel 69, 79–80, 89–91, 118–19
France 13
  empire 54
  historical community in 2, 28, 30–1
  influence in Latin America 8, 31
  invasion of Mexico 8
Franco, Francisco 30
Frank, Andre Gunder 47–8
French, William E. 83, 89
Freyre, Gilberto 26, 52, 110–11
Friedman, Milton 48
frontiers 97–8

Games, Alison 106
Gamio, Manuel 58
Gaos, José 29
García Canclini, Néstor 89
García Icazbalceta, Joaquín 22
Geertz, Clifford 89
gender and women's history 67–70, 89–92, 99, 119
Genovese, Eugene 52–3
gentlemen scholars 3, 20, 121
geography 113
Gibson, Charles 33–4, 57, 59, 113
Gilroy, Paul 109
globalization 76–7, 89, 101, 102, 104
Godinho, Vitorino Magalhães 30
Gootenberg, Paul 104
Gortari, Eli de 115
Graham, Richard 73
Gramsci, Antonio 79, 84, 90
Grandin, Greg 103
Great Britain
  empire 16, 49, 54, 81, 123
  historical community in 2–3, 28, 31, 38, 73–4, 77, 91, 123
Great Depression 49, 75, 124
Great Recession 77
Griffith, William J. 27
Gruzinski, Serge 71, 92
Guardino, Peter 85
Guerra, François-Xavier 87–8
Gunther, John 14
Gutierrez, Ramon 99
Guy, Donna 69

Haber, Stephen 105
Habermas, Jürgen 86–7
Hackett, Charles W. 27
Haiti 11, 13, 55, 56
Hamäläinen, Pekka 99
Hamilton, Earl J. 40, 63, 106
Handbook of Latin American Studies 25

Hanke, Lewis 32
Haring, Clarence 26, 34
Harvard University 26, 34, 68, 106
Hassig, Ross 93
Hawthorne, Walter 109
Hennessy, Alistair 31
Herring, Hubert 13, 14
Heywood, Linda 109
Hispanic American Historical Review (HAHR) 9, 13, 25, 73, 82–4
Hispanic Foundation 34
Hobsbawm, Eric 83
Holanda, Sérgio Buarque de 26
Humphries, Robin 31
hybridity 107, 116

immigration 17, 97, 102
imperialism 8, 44, 47, 103, 116, 118
  cultural 13
  ecological 113
Incas 59
independence
  wars 7–8, 22, 65–6, 83, 88, 94
Indians/Native Americans/indigenous peoples 8, 12, 17, 40, 57–9, 108, 111, 117
  indigenism 23, 93–4
  languages 93
  origin of name 6
  rebellions 94
Indies (*las Indias*) 6, 20
indigenous history 33–4, 92–4, 97–9
industrialization 65, 75
Inquisition 68, 84, 91, 117
institutions 70–3
  historical 22–3
  scientific 116, 118
  universities 25, 30, 36, 53, 77, 110, 121, 124

intellectual history 32, 88, 101–2
Irving, Washington 20
Israel 6

James, C. L. R. 56
James, Daniel 70
Jiménez Moreno, Wigberto 58
Jobet, Julio César 44
Johns Hopkins University 32, 54, 106, 109, 110
Johnson, John J. 46
Johnson, Lyndon 45
Joseph, Gilbert 85, 102
Joslin, David 31
Journal of Latin American Studies 73

Keen, Benjamin 15, 21, 23, 24, 73
Kennedy, John F. 45
Kings College London 31
Kiple, Kenneth 56
Klein, Herbert S. 56, 109
Knight, Franklin 56
Kristeva, Julia 69

labor 63–7
  history 66–7
  rural 61
land tenure systems 60–1
Landers, Jane 108
Lanning, John Tate 27, 32
Las Casas, Bartolomé de 19, 32
Latin America
  colonial period 19–20, 33, 106, 117, 120
  critiques of term 12–13, 121–2
  definitions 15–17, 55, 78, 125–6
  graduate programs in 38, 116
  historical community in

38, 73–4, 77, 85, 91, 94, 96–7, 125
  literature 37, 93
  origins of term 5–18
  post-colonial period 33
  universities 20, 77, 96
  various names for 7
Latin American and Caribbean Society of Environmental History/La Sociedad Latinoamericana y Caribeña de Historia Ambiental (SOLCHA) 115
Latin American Perspectives 49
Latin American Research Review 12
Latin American studies 10, 125
  boom in 4, 12, 36–7, 121
  centers 10–11
Latin American Studies Association (LASA) 12
Latin culture 9
latinoamericanos 11
Latinx/Chicano studies 99, 100
Lavrin, Asunción 68
legal history 72–3
Lenin, V. I. 47
Leonard, Irving A. 27
León-Portilla, Miguel 58
Lévi-Strauss, Claude 42, 80
Levy, Maria Bárbara 42
linguistics 42, 78, 93
Lockhart, James 57–8, 92–3
longue durée 31
Lorente, Sebastián 22
Lummis, Charles F. 21
Lynch, John 31

Malinche, La/Doña Marina 68
Mallon, Florencia 59, 84, 85
Marchant, Alexander 32
Marcilio, Maria Luiza 42
Mariátegui, José Carlos 44
Marshall, T. H. 88

Martin, Cheryl 89
Martin, Percy Alvin 13, 33
Martínez, Oscar 100
Martínez-Alier (Stolcke), Verena 69
Marx, Karl 43, 80
Marxism 43–9, 52–3, 69, 79, 84, 91
Matory, Lorand 109
Matos Moctezuma, Eduardo 59
Mattoso, Kátia de Queirós 53–4
Mauro, Frédéric 42–3
McCaa, Robert 40
Mecham, John Lloyd 27
medicine, history of 104, 115–19
Melville, Elinor 113
Memmi, Albert 81
Menchu, Rigoberta 69
merchants 63–6
Mesoamerica 58, 60, 61, 92–4
mestizaje/mestiçagem 26, 29, 110–12
Mexican Revolution 25, 29, 33, 62
Mexico
  graduate programs in 2, 25
  historical community in 28–30, 34
  immigration 17
  Institutional Revolutionary Party (PRI) 29
  racial categories 12
  relations with U.S. 33
Middle East 76, 103, 110
Mignolo, Walter 13, 122
Miller, Joseph 109
mining 113, 114
  gold 63–4
  silver 61, 63–4
Mitre, Bartolomé 22
modernization theory 45, 116
Moreno, Gabriel René 22

Moreno Fraginals, Manuel 56
Morgan, Lewis Henry 21
Morse, Richard 32
Moses, Bernard 23–4
Mott, Luiz 91
Moya, José 10
multiculturalism 93
Munro, Dana G. 14
Murra, John 59
music 89, 104

Nahuatl 57–8, 92–3
Napoleon III 8
Nash, June 58
National Research Council 10
nationalism and national identity 83, 101
  Brazil 29
  Mexico 29, 85
  Peru 85
négritude 111
neo-liberalism 75–7, 84, 104–5
New World 6, 16, 20, 24
Newson, Linda 40
norteamericanos 11
North, Douglass 105
Nugent, Daniel 85

O'Donnell, Guillermo 72
Old World 6, 16
oral history 69–70
Oswaldo Cruz Foundation 118

Palomino, Pablo 104
Pan American movement 24
Patterson, Orlando 109
Peace Corps 37
peasants 61–2, 85
Pease, Franklin 59
peninsulares 7, 72
Pérez Brignoli, Héctor 43
Perkins, Dexter 24
Perón, Juan 67
Philippines 24

Piccato, Pablo 87
Pilcher, Jeffrey 89
Pinochet, Augusto 76
political history 71–2, 84–5, 94
political science 51
popular culture 88–9
populism 67
Portugal 13
  empire 16, 22, 31, 46–7, 63, 65
  historical community in 2, 28, 30
positivism 20–1
post-colonial studies 78–81, 116
post-modernism 78–81, 102
post-structuralism 78–81
Potosí 61, 63–4
Prado Júnior, Caio 26, 44
Pratt, Mary Louise 103
Prébisch, Raúl 47
Prescott, William Hickling 20–2, 24, 27
Price, Richard 56
Priestley, Herbert I. 27
Protestantism 24, 32
public health, history of 91, 104, 115–19
public sphere 85–8
Puerto Rico 11, 17, 55

quantitative history 31, 39–43, 109, 118
Quipu 119

race/ethnicity 110–12, 118
  race relations 51–7, 104, 111
  racial categories 7
  racial mixture 24, 29, 110–11; *see also mestizaje/ mestiçagem*
Ramos, Raúl 99
Randall, Margaret 69
Ranke, Leopold von 20, 23, 28–30

Reagan, Ronald 75
Redfield, Robert 58, 62
Reis, João José 54
religion/religious beliefs 71, 109
religious orders and institutions 68, 72, 89
Reséndez, Andrés 99
Restall, Matthew 93
Ricard, Robert 70–1
Richardson, David 109
Rippy, J. Fred 14, 27
Riva Palacio, Vicente 22
Robertson, William 22
Robertson, William Spence 13, 24, 25
Rockefeller Foundation 117
Romano, Ruggiero 64
romanticism 20, 93
Romero, José Luis 30
Ross, Stanley 33
Rostow, W. W. 45
rural history 60–2
Russell-Wood, A. J. R. 54

Sabato, Hilda 86–7
Safier, Neil 116
Said, Edward 81
St. John, Rachel 100
Salazar, Antonio de Oliveira 30
Sandinistas 69, 76
Santiago, Myrna 114
Santo Domingo 20
Scarano, Francisco 56
Schaeffer, Wendell G. 14
Schoultz, Lars 103
Schroeder, Susan 93
Schwartz, Stuart 54, 62, 117
science, history of 104, 115–19
Scott, Joan 89–90
Scott, Rebecca J. 56
Second World War 2, 9, 25, 44, 49, 58
Seed, Patricia 69, 107
Seigel, Micol 104

Senghor, Léopold 111
Seville 26, 63
sexuality *see* gender and women's history
Shining Path 84
Simonian, Lane 114
Simpson, Lesley Byrd 24, 33, 40
Skidmore, Thomas E. 15
slavery 6–7, 51–7, 107
 Brazil 40, 52–4, 61
 Caribbean 52, 54–7, 61
 resistance to 56, 62
 slave trade 7, 56, 102, 108–10
 United States 41, 52
Smith, Peter H. 15, 103
Smithsonian Institution 10
Social Darwinism 24
social history 31, 33, 37, 39, 43, 51–74, 90, 94, 98, 111, 123
Social Science Research Council 25, 37
socialism 46–7, 61, 76, 82
Sociedad Latinoamericana de Historia de las Ciencias y la Tecnología 119
Society for Latin American Studies 12, 73
Society for the History of Technology (SHOT) 119
sociology 48, 51, 78, 79
Soto Laveaga, Gabriela 100
Southey, Robert 22
Souza, Laura de Mello e 64, 91
Soviet Union (USSR) 9, 44–5, 82
Spain 13
 empire 10, 16, 46–7, 54, 63, 65, 94
 historical community in 2, 28
Spalding, Hobart 67

Spalding, Karen 59
Spencer, Herbert 21
Spivak, Gayatri 81–2
Stanford University 27, 105
Stavenhagen, Rodolf 62
Stein, Barbara 48
Stein, Stanley 34, 40, 48
Stepan, Nancy 116, 118
Stern, Steve 59, 90
Street, John 31
structuralism 31, 42, 71, 80
subalterns 79, 81–2, 83, 84–5

Tandeter, Enrique 64
Tannenbaum, Frank 33, 52
Tavárez, David 93
Tax, Sol 58
Taylor, William 72
technology, history of 119
Tenorio-Trillo, Mauricio 122
Terraciano, Kevin 93
textbooks 13–14, 73
Thatcher, Margaret 75, 77
Third World 44–5
Thompson, E. P. 91
Thornton, John 109
Tinker Foundation 37
Topik, Steven 105
Toplin, Robert Brent 54
Torre, Raúl Haya de la 93–4
Townsend, Camilla 93
transnational history 17, 100–4, 120, 122
Truett, Samuel 100
Tupac Amaru 94
Tupac Catari 94

UNESCO 11
United Kingdom *see* Great Britain
United Nations 11
United States
  Department of Education 5, 37
  Department of State 46
  graduate programs in 2, 36, 38–9, 110, 116, 123
  historical community in 38, 73–4, 77, 85, 91, 94, 96–7, 121–5
  National Defense Education Act 9–10, 36
  national resource centers 10–11
  relations with Latin America 24, 69, 102–4
Universidad Nacional Autónoma de México (UNAM) 62
Universidade de São Paulo (USP) 42, 53
University of California, Berkeley 21, 23, 24, 25, 27, 63, 113
  Berkeley School 33–4, 40, 58, 118
University of Chicago 48, 62
University of Hull 109
University of New Mexico 98
University of Paris 43, 53, 59, 62, 64, 87
University of Texas 26–7
University of Wisconsin 109
USSR *see* Soviet Union

Vainfas, Ronaldo 91
Valcárcel, Luis 59
Van Young, Eric 62, 82–4, 94
Vargas, Getúlio 67
Vasconcelos, José 110
Vespucci, Amerigo 6
Viezzer, Moema 69–70

Wachtel, Nathan 59
Wakild, Emily 114
Waldseemüller, Martin 6
Wasserman, Mar 73

Weber, David J., 98–9
West, Robert C. 63
Whitaker, Arthur P. 24
White, Richard 99
Williams, Eric 57
Williamson, Edwin 15
Wolf, Eric 62
Womack, Jr., John 62

women's movements and feminism, 68, 69, 90
Worcester, Donald E. 14

Yale University 23, 26, 34, 53

Zavala, Silvio 29
Zolov, Eric 89